Animal and Wildlife

Coloring Book for Adults

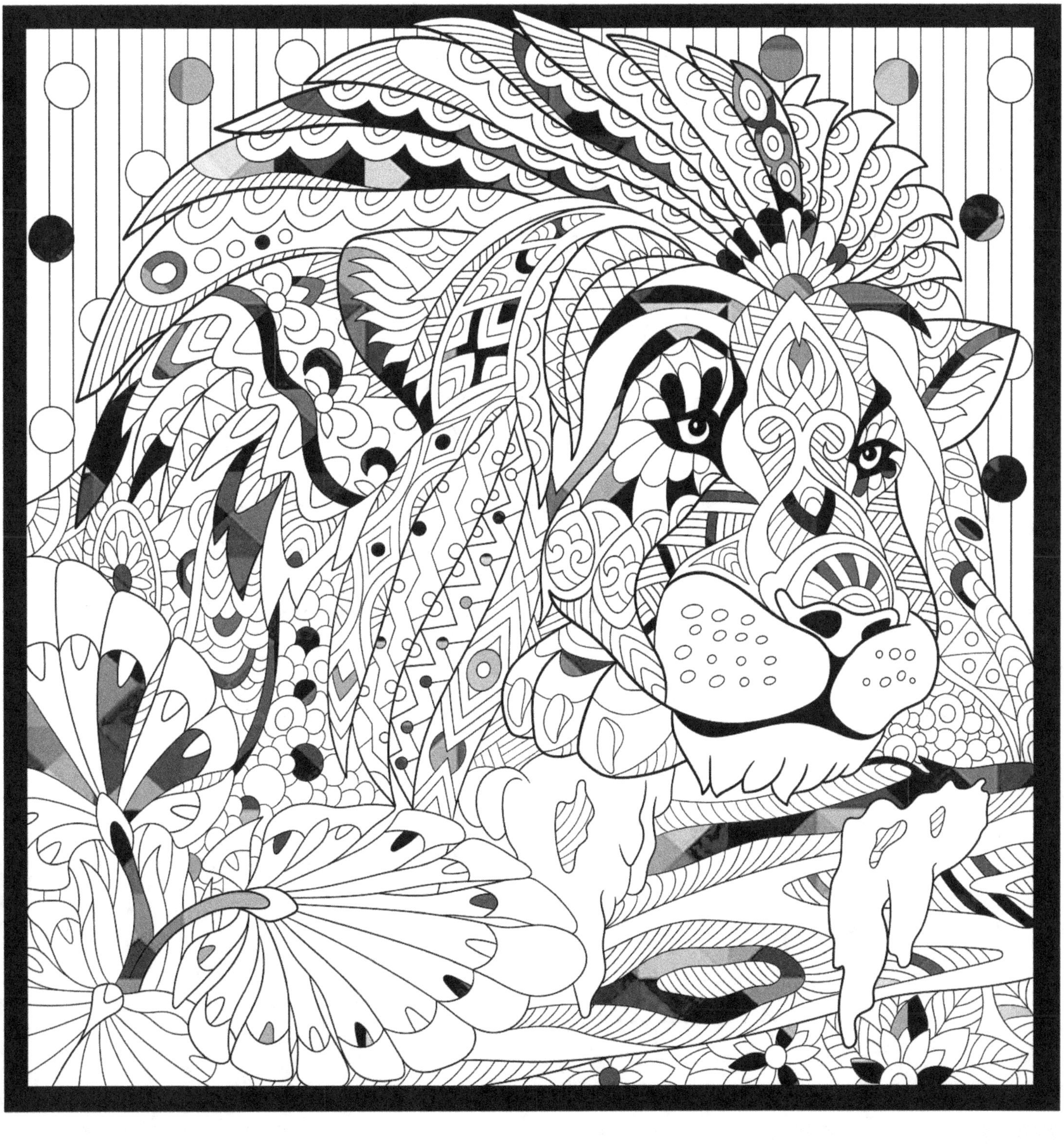

TEST YOUR COLOR

TEST YOUR COLOR

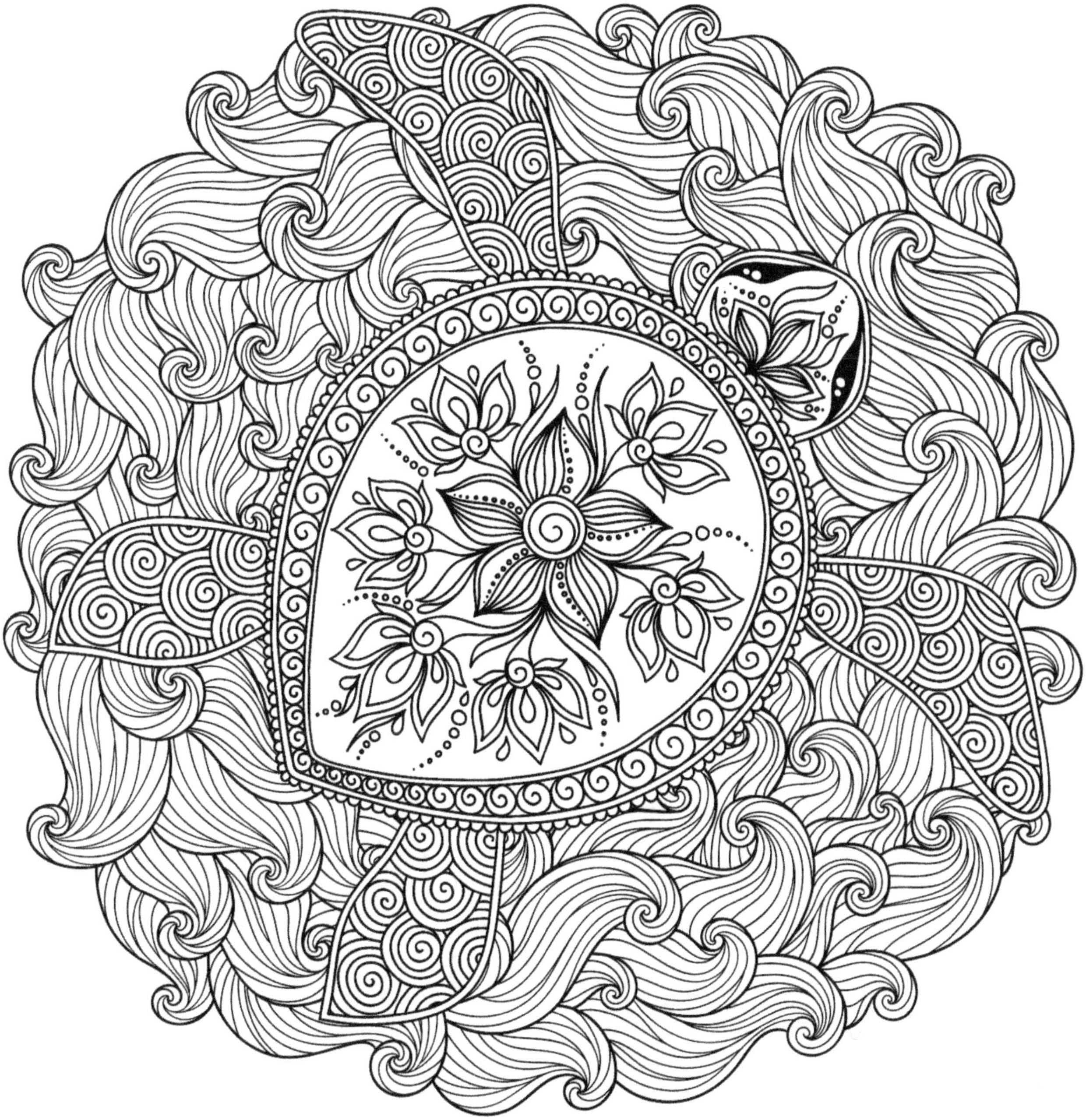

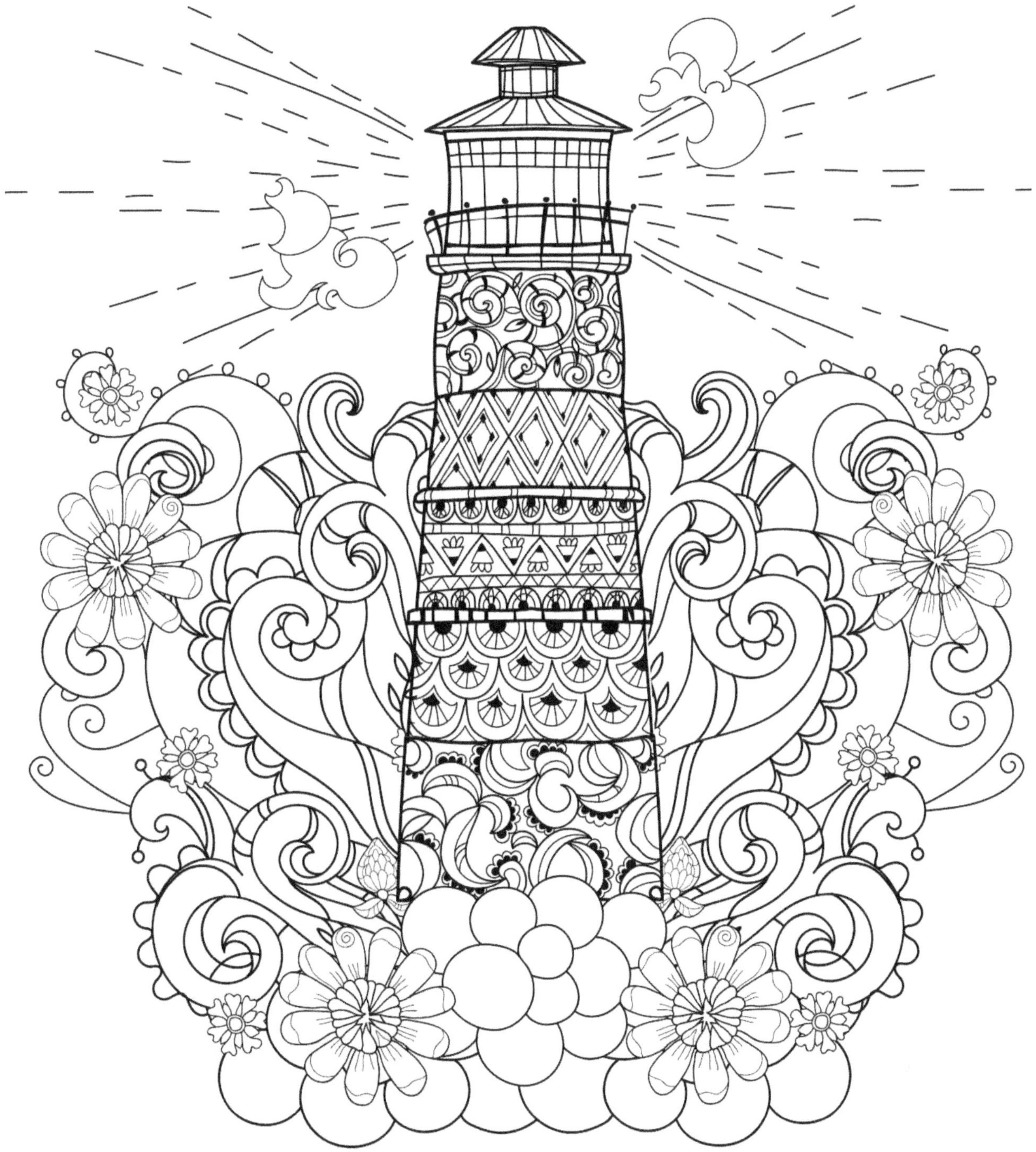

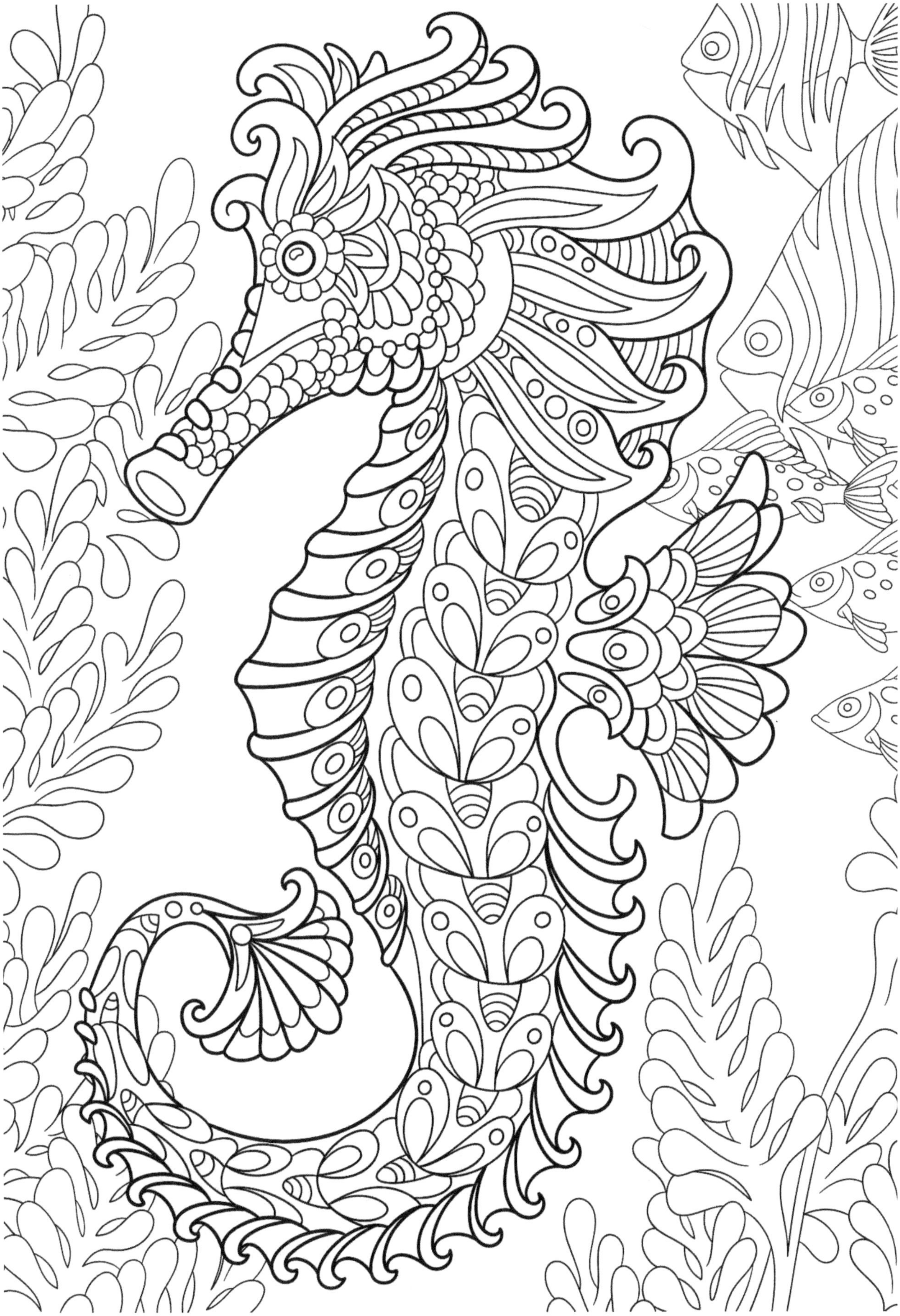

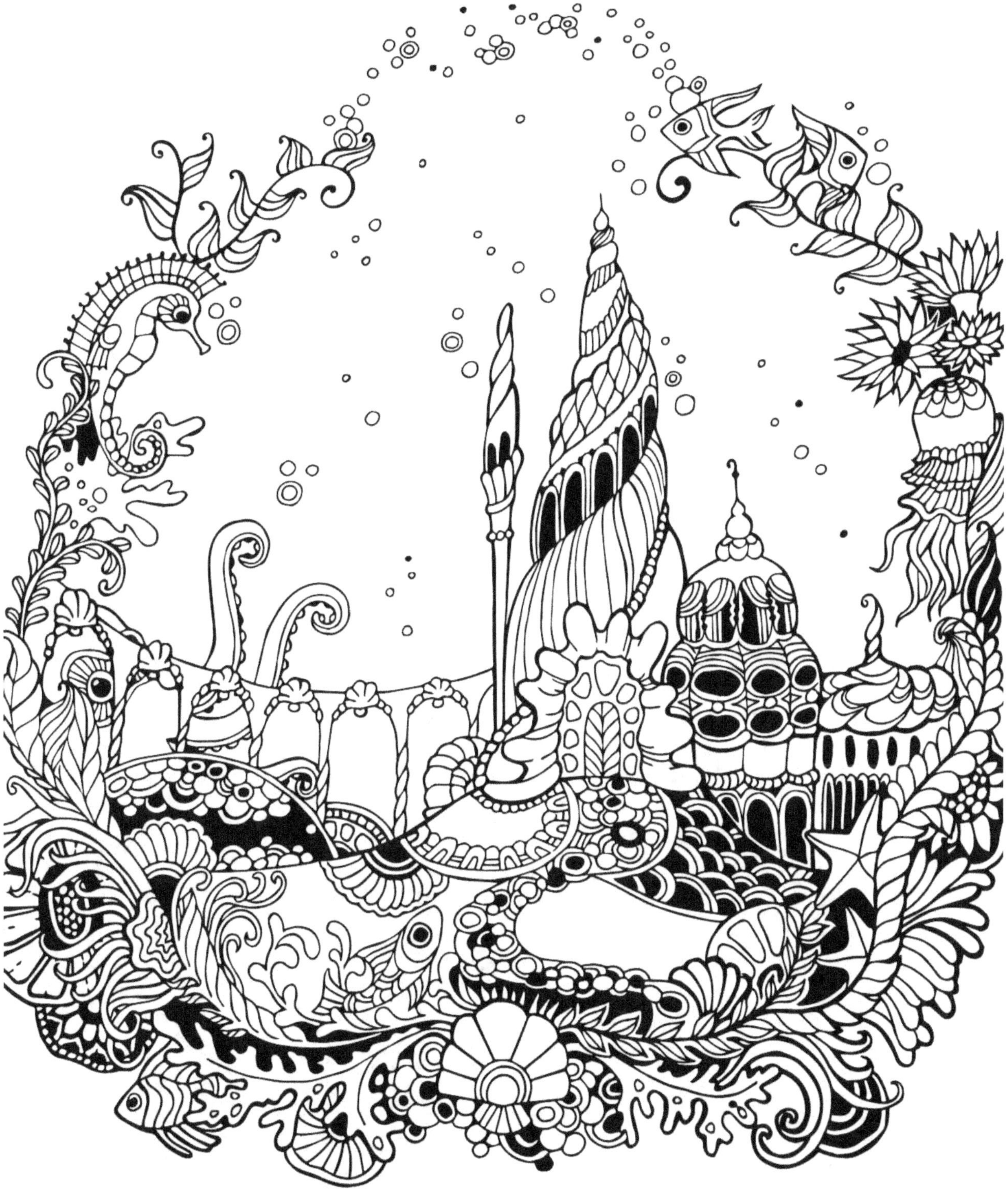

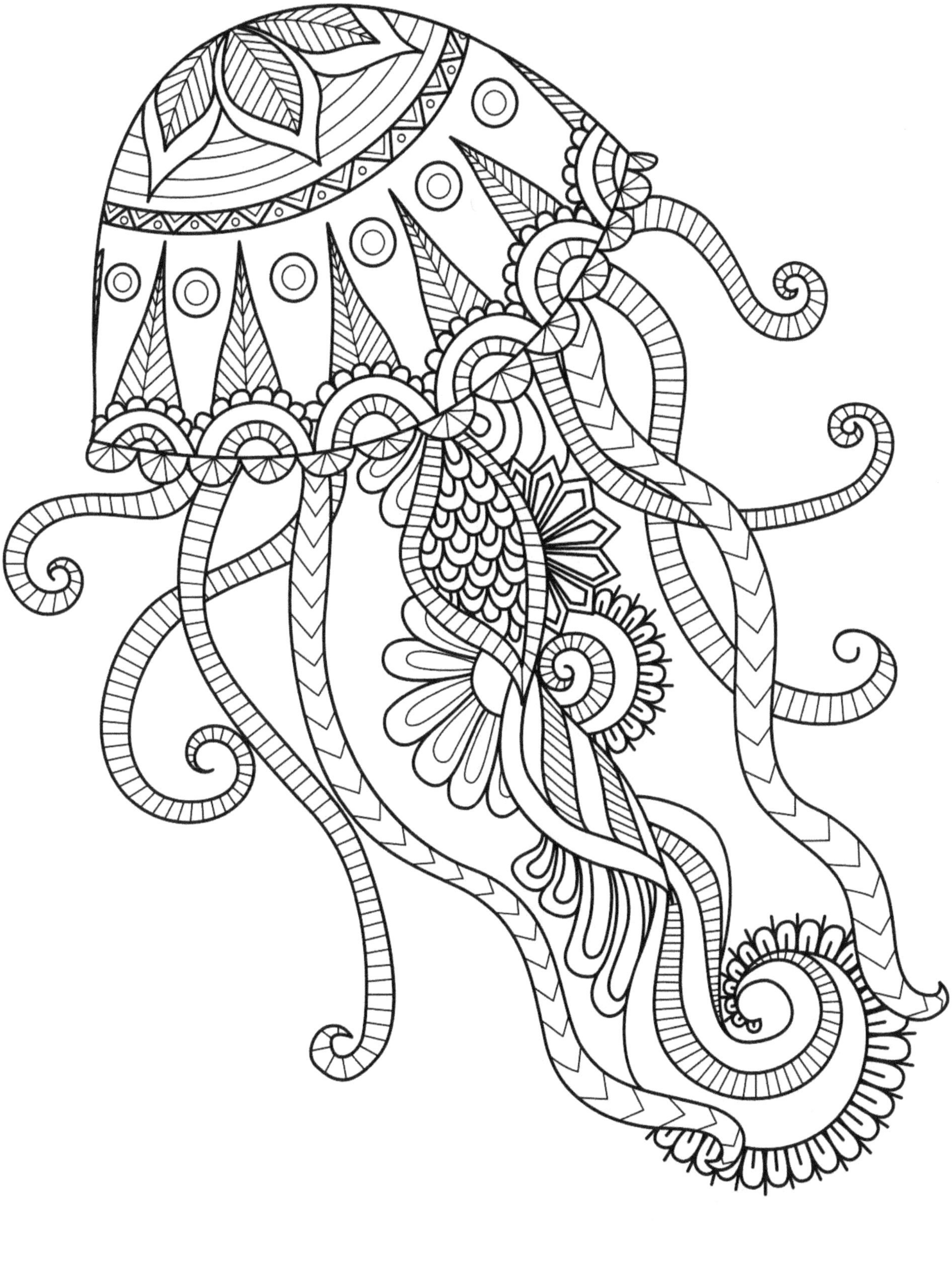

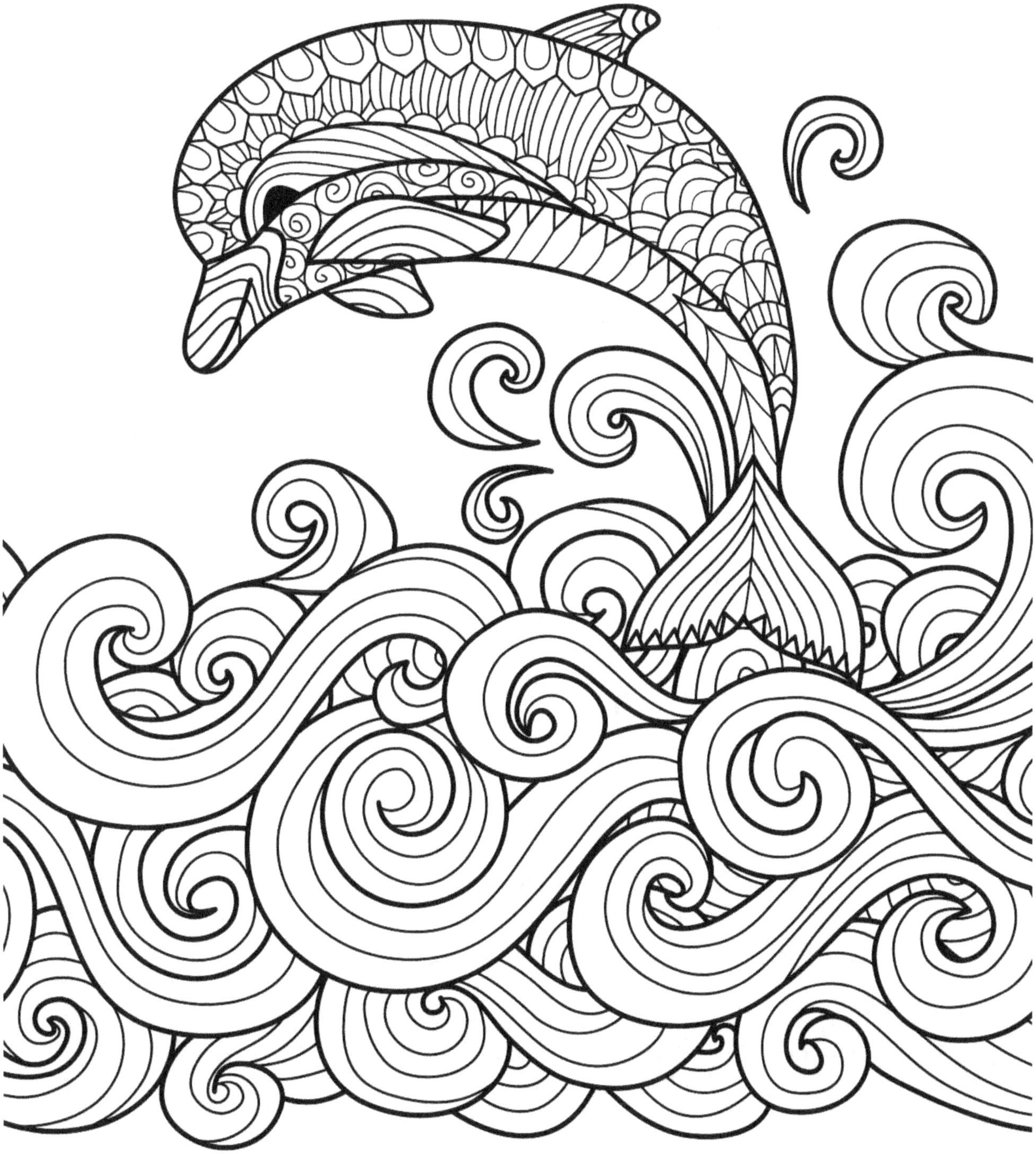

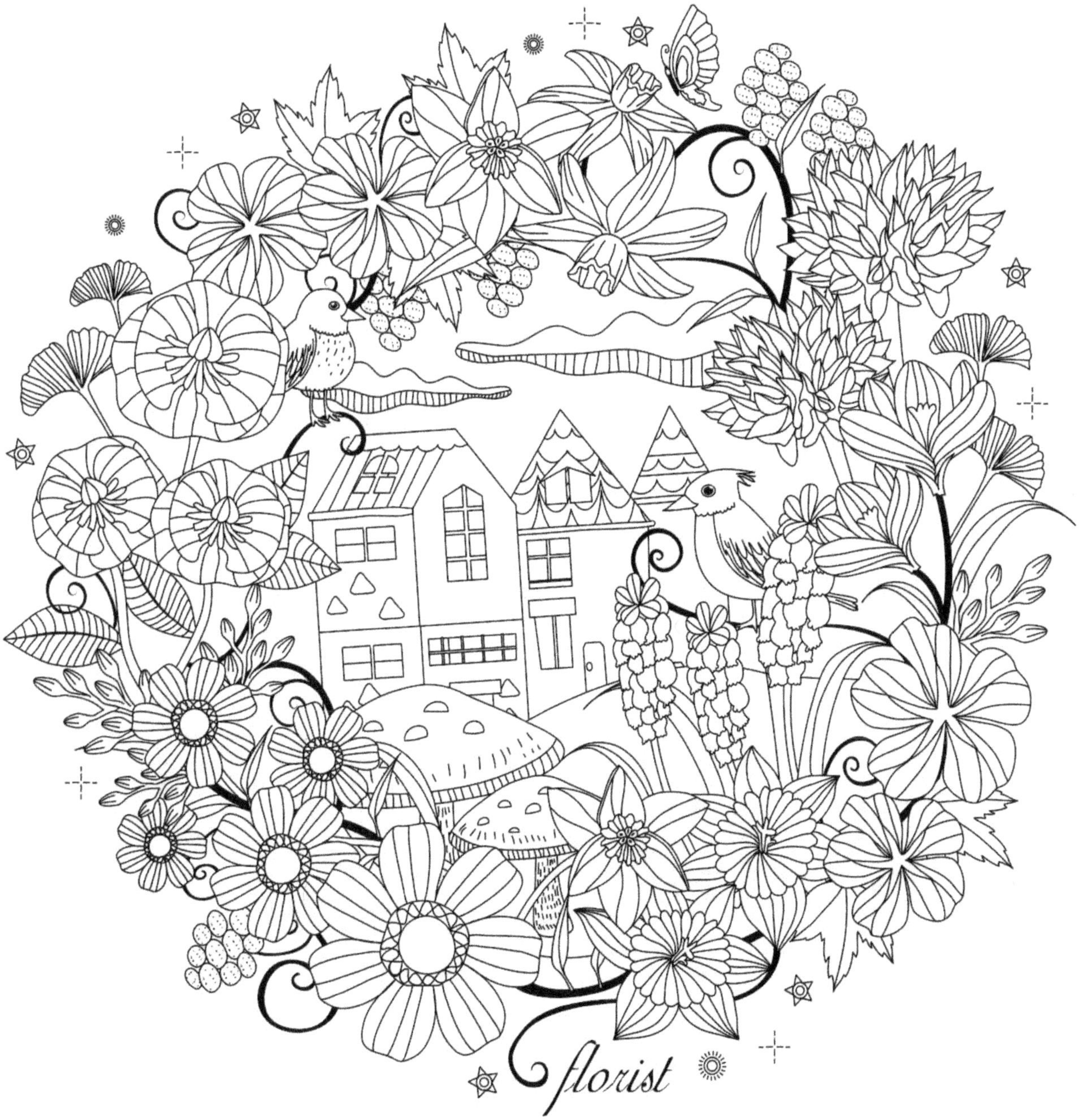
florist

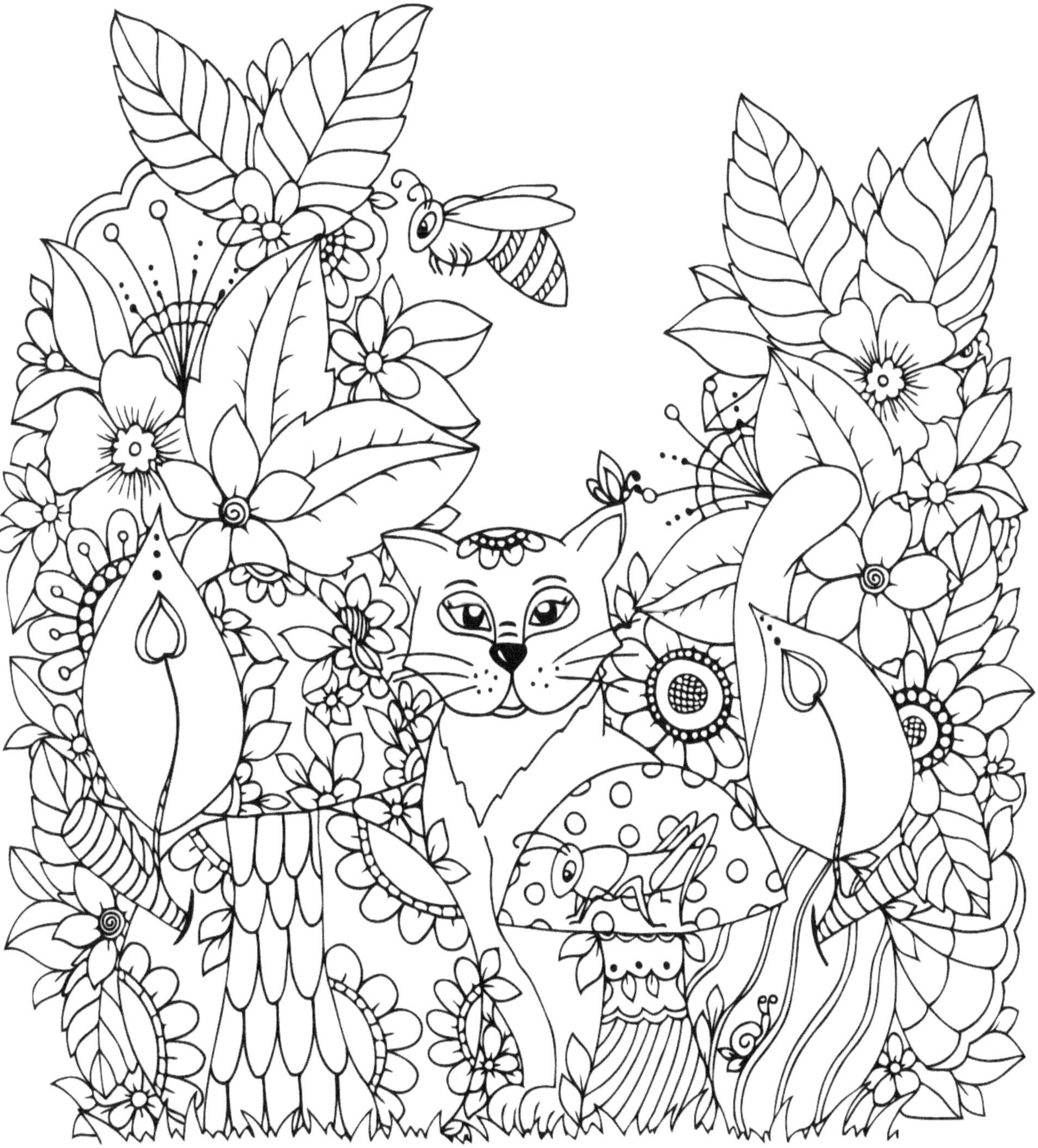

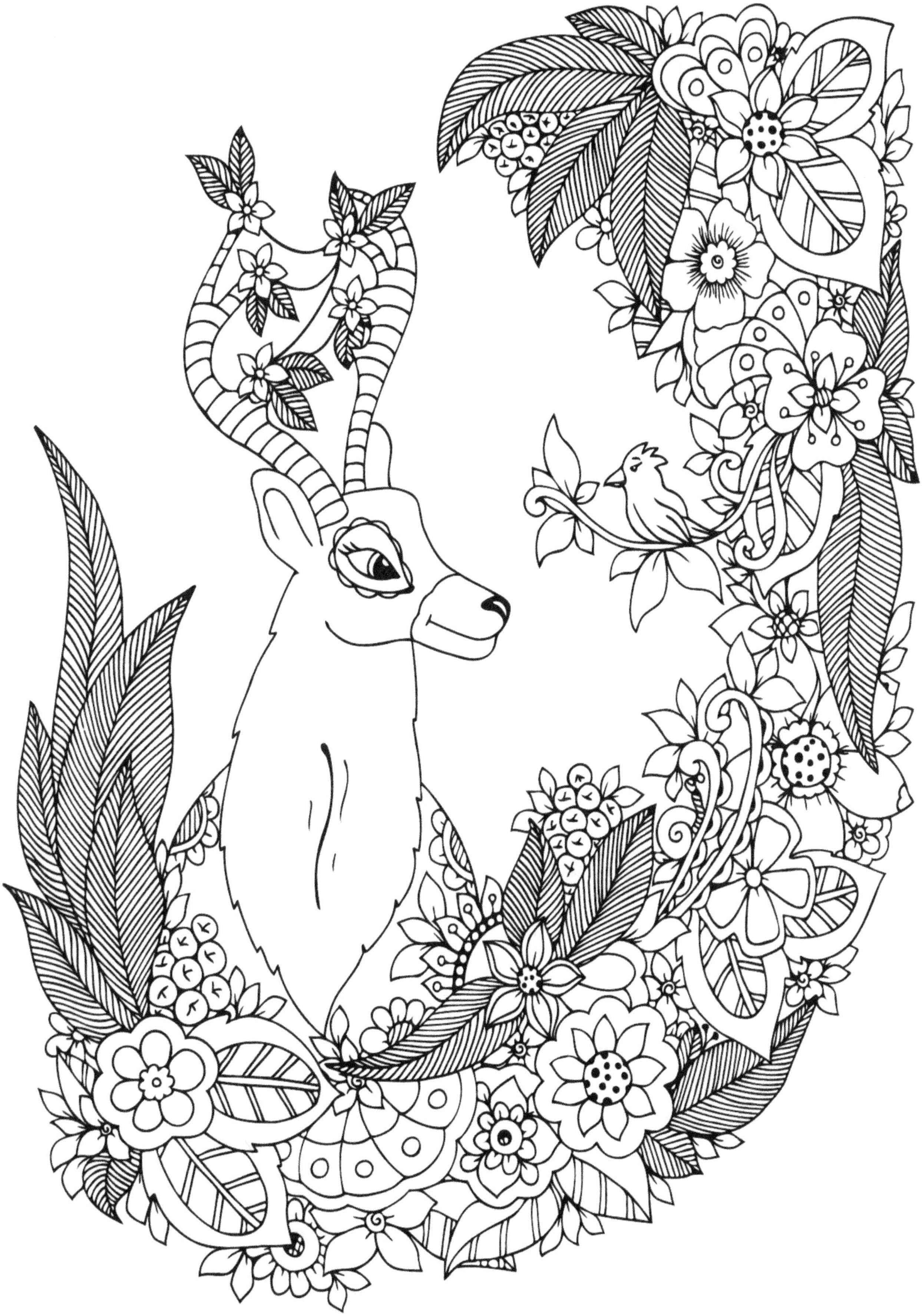

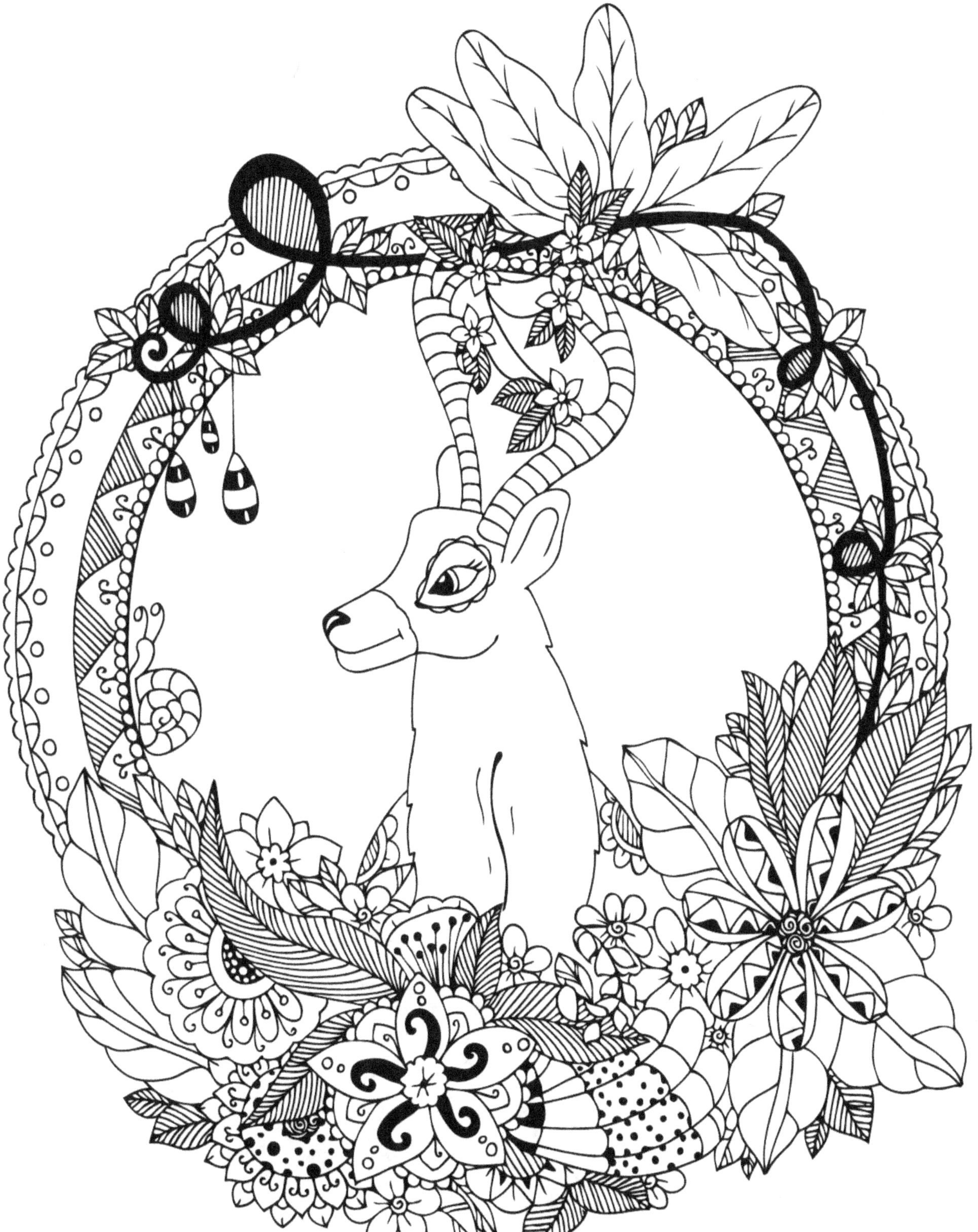

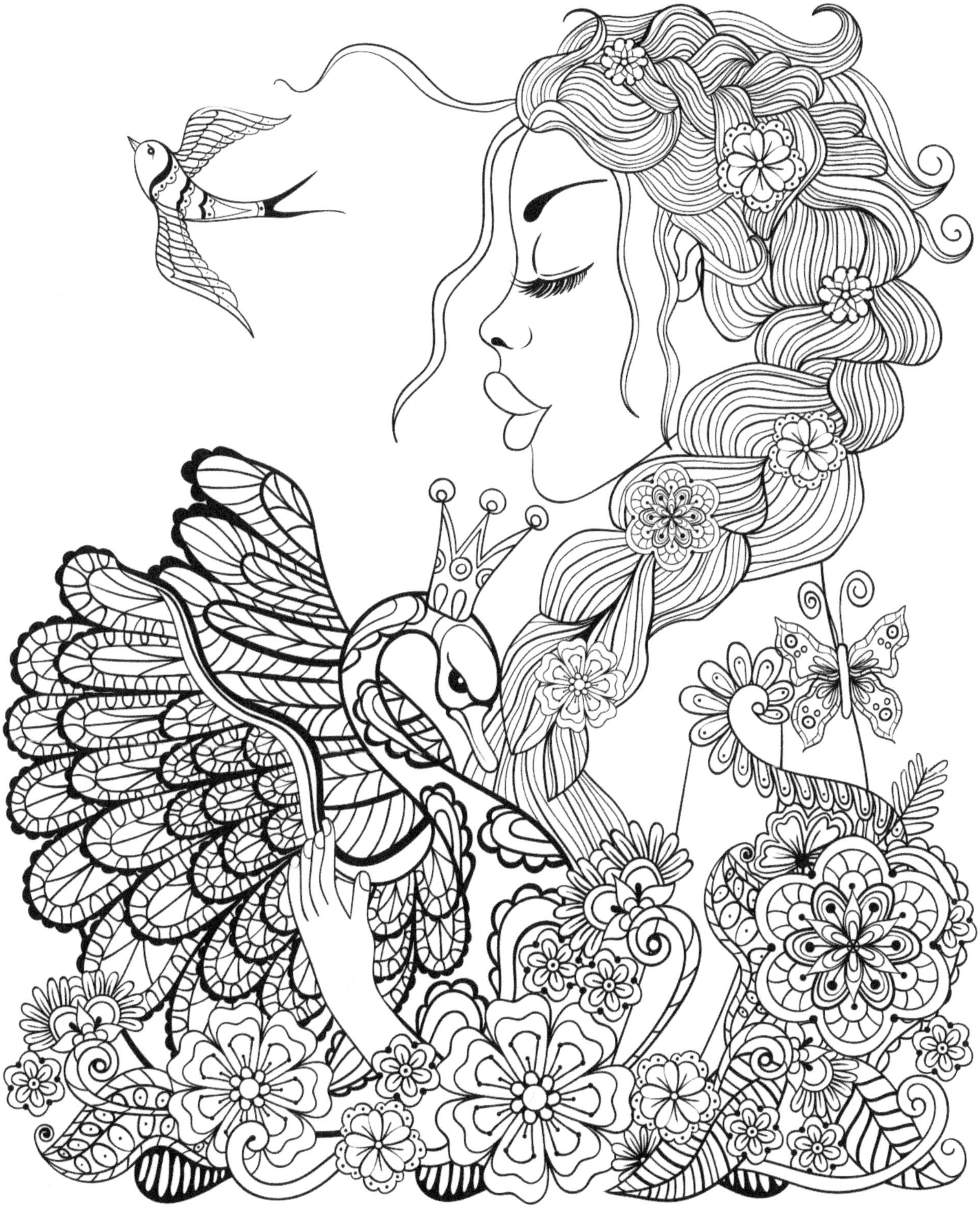

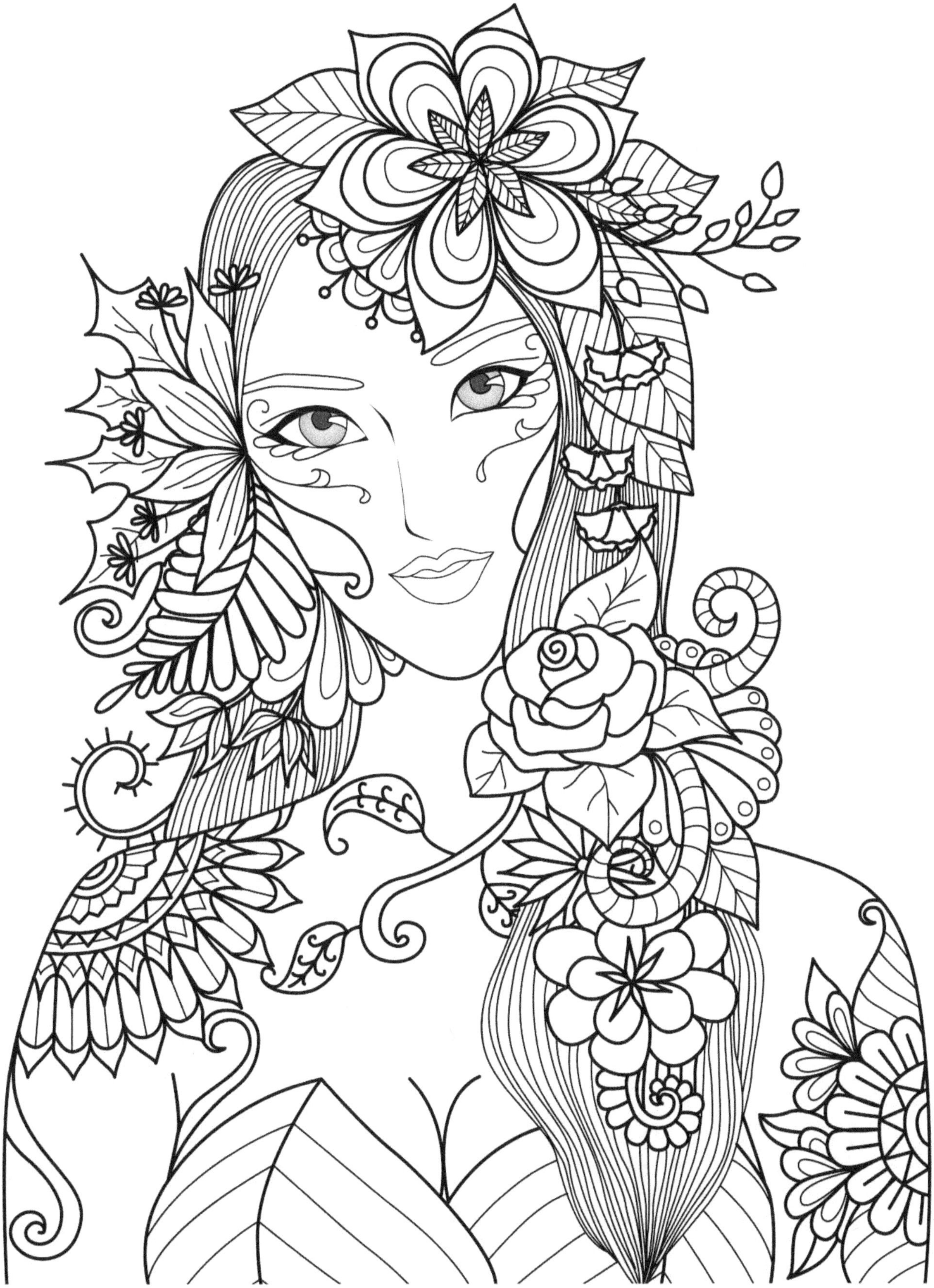

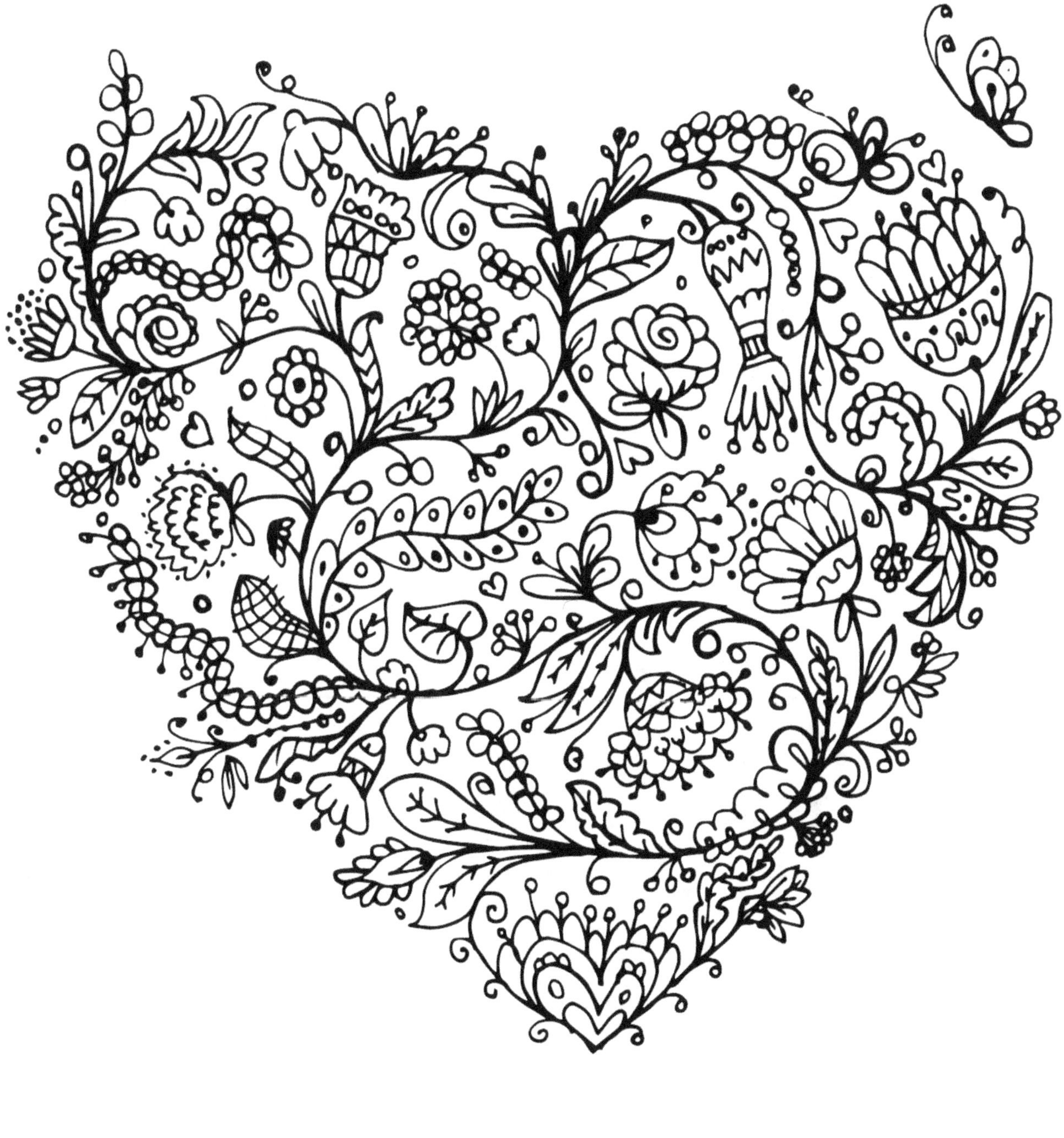

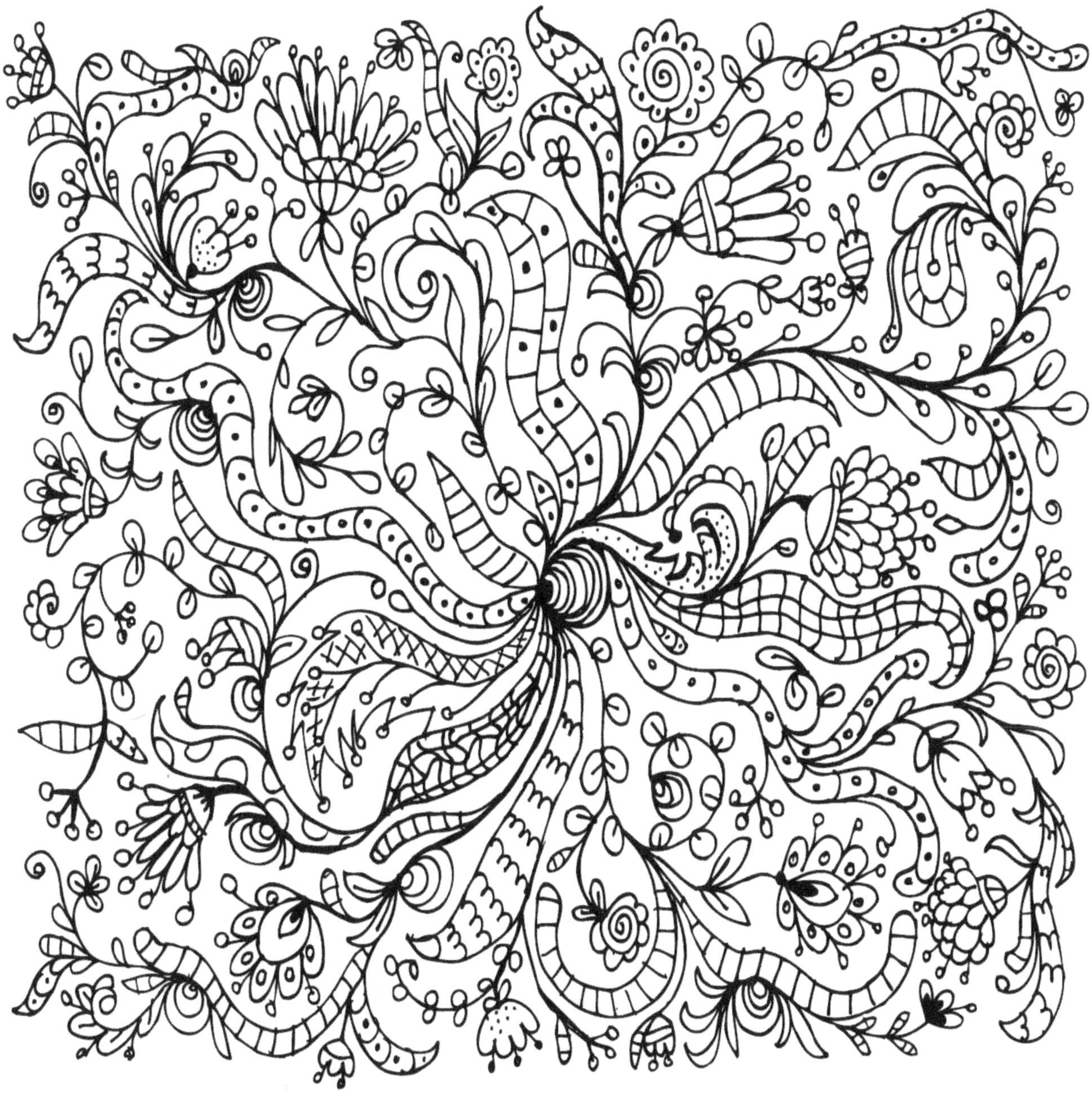

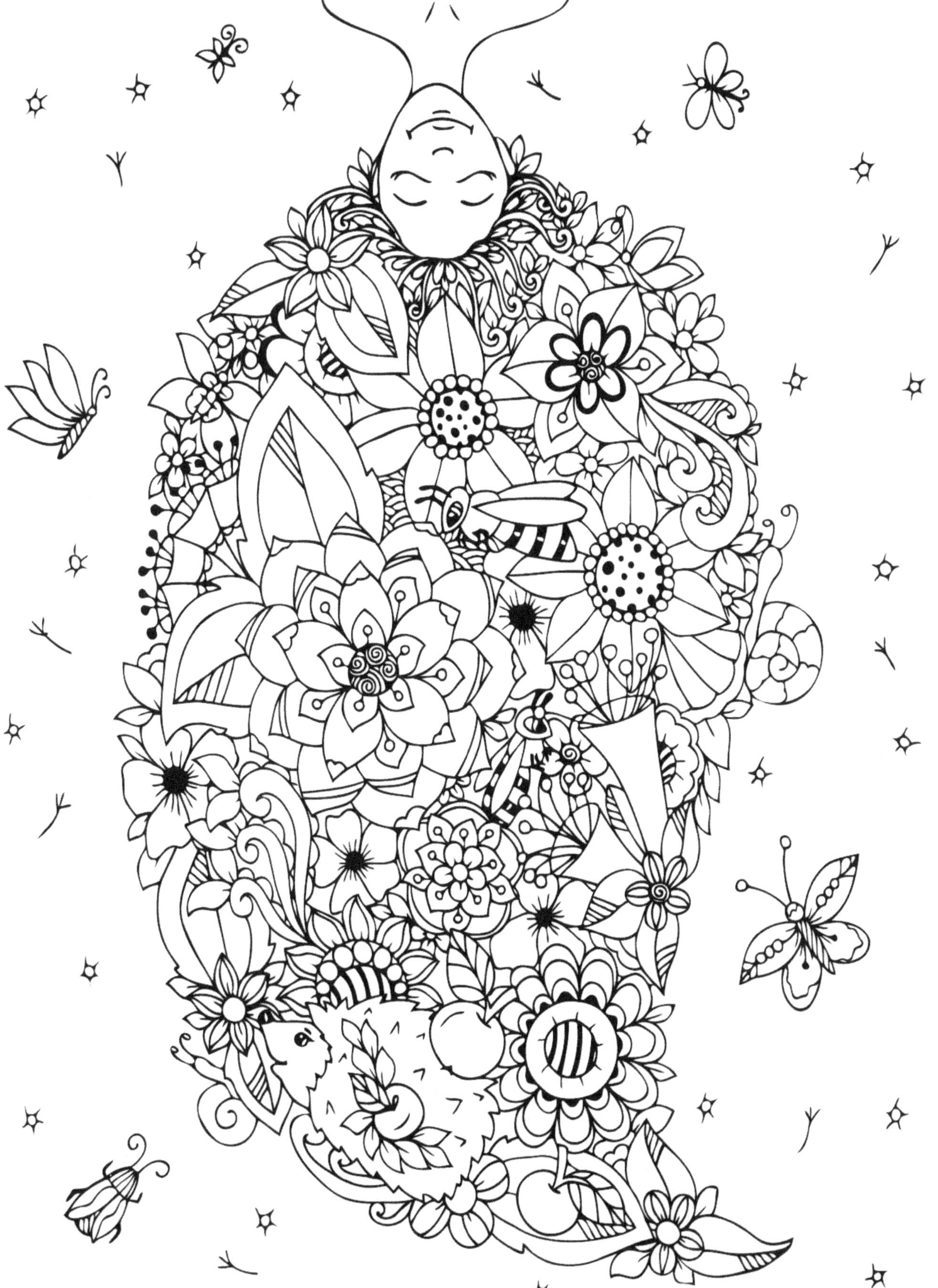

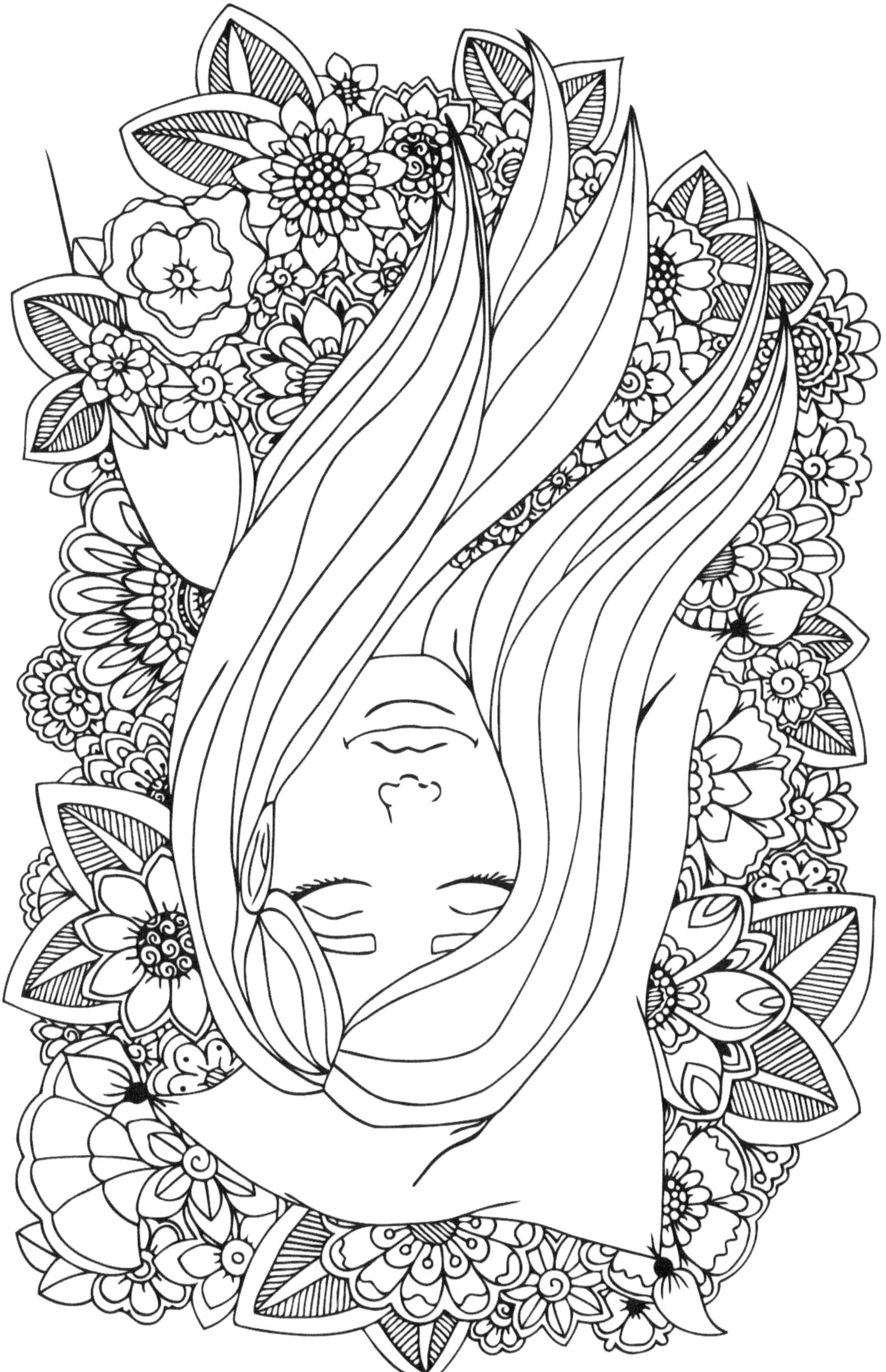

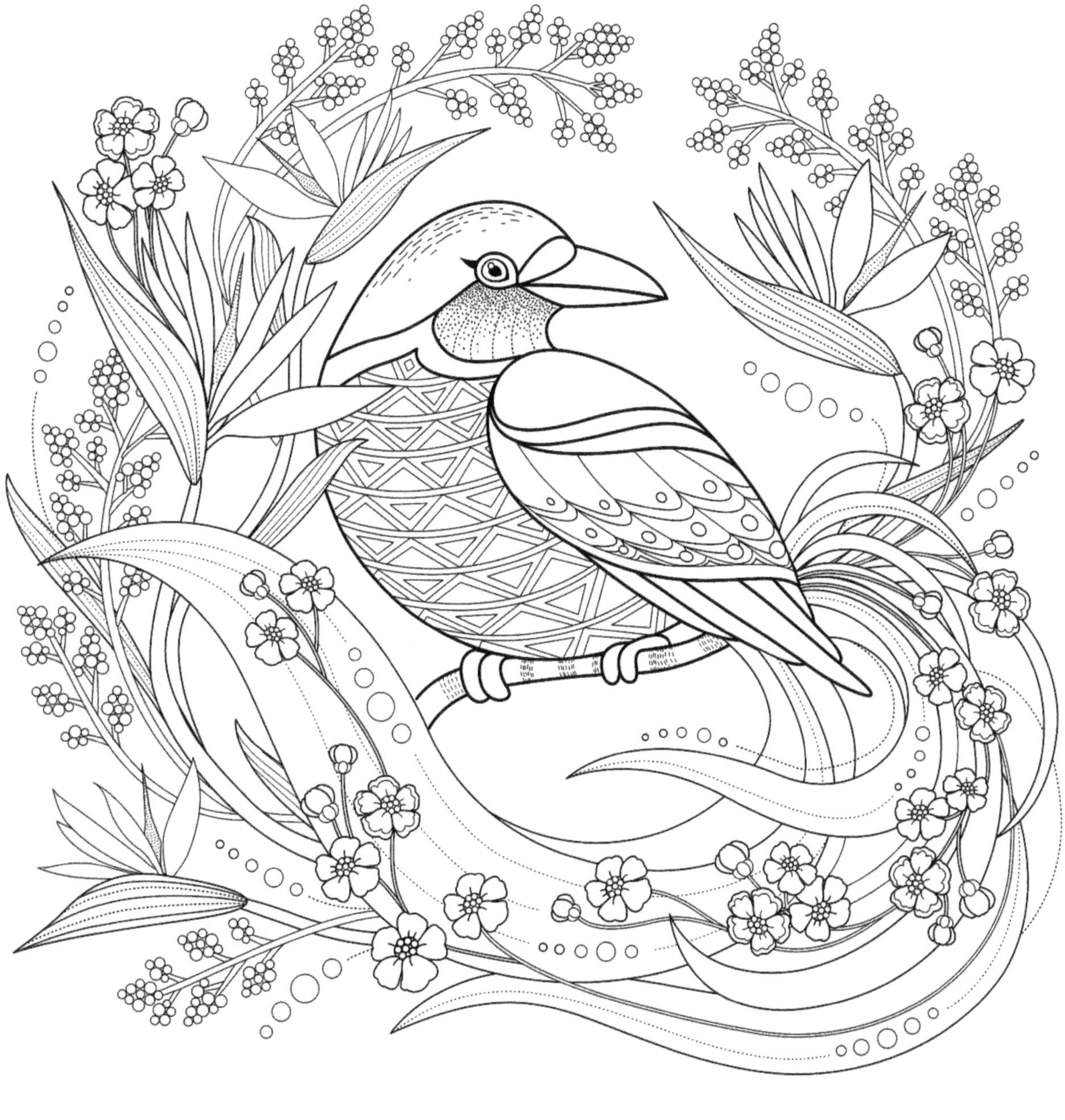

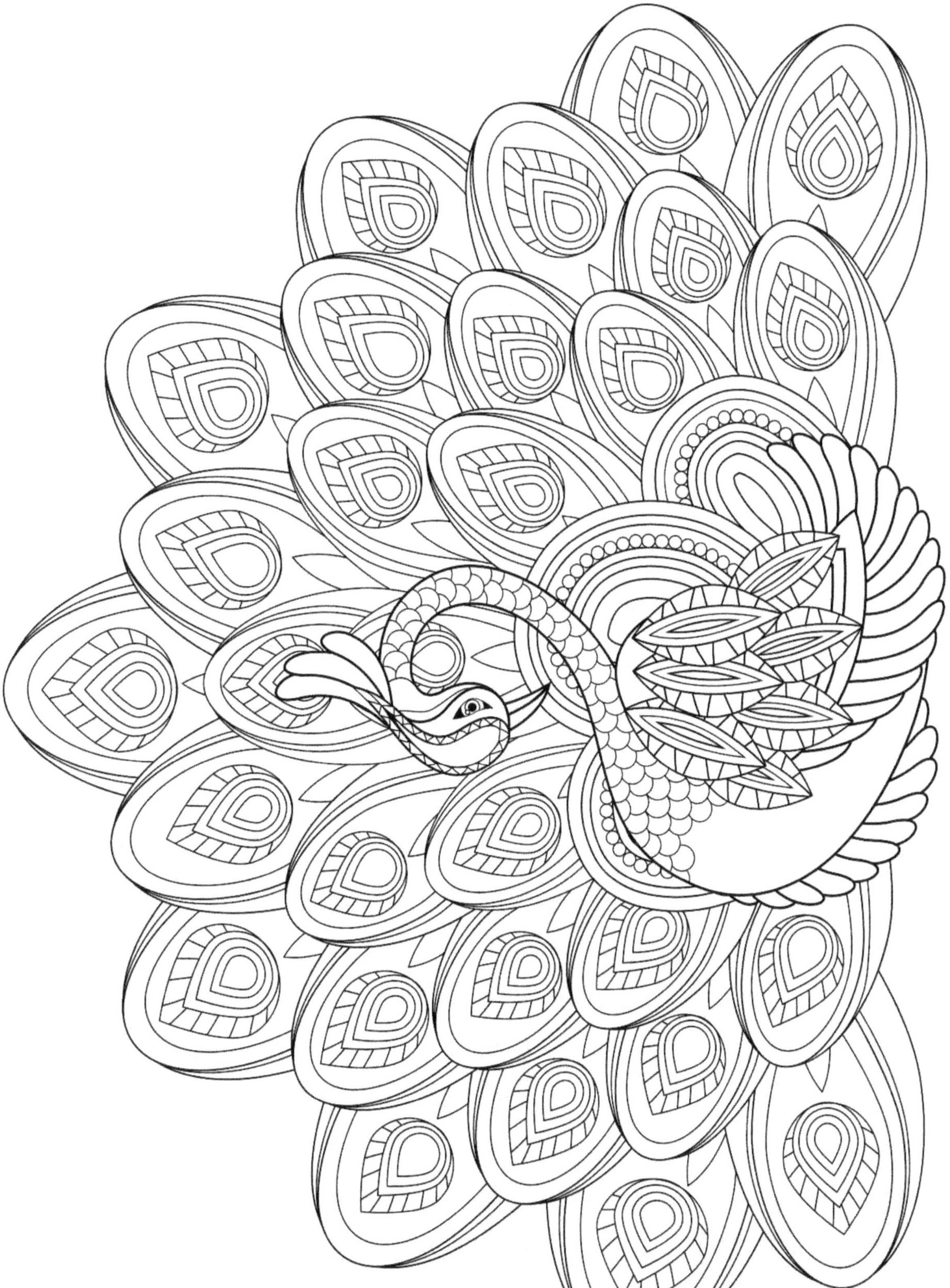

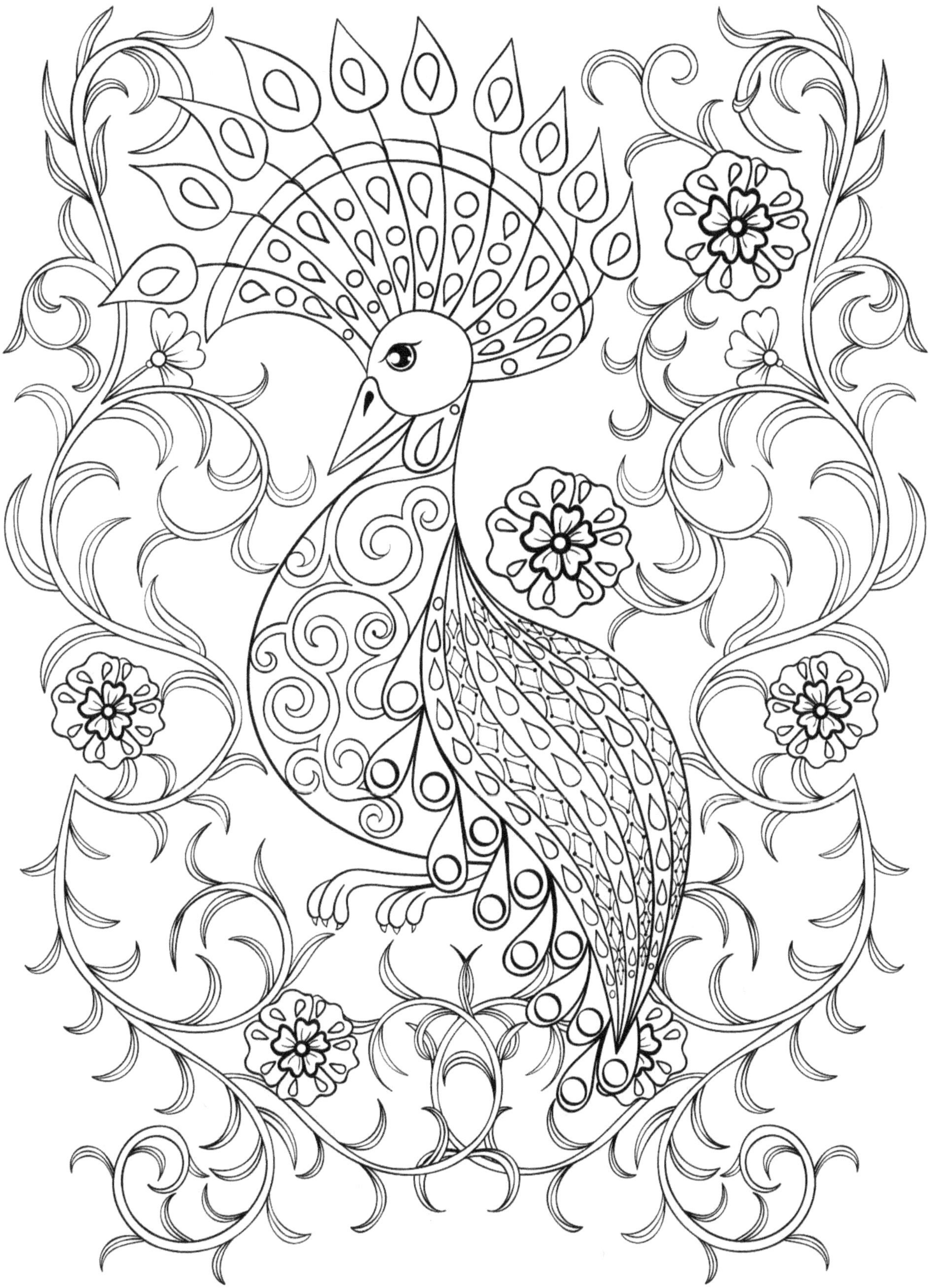

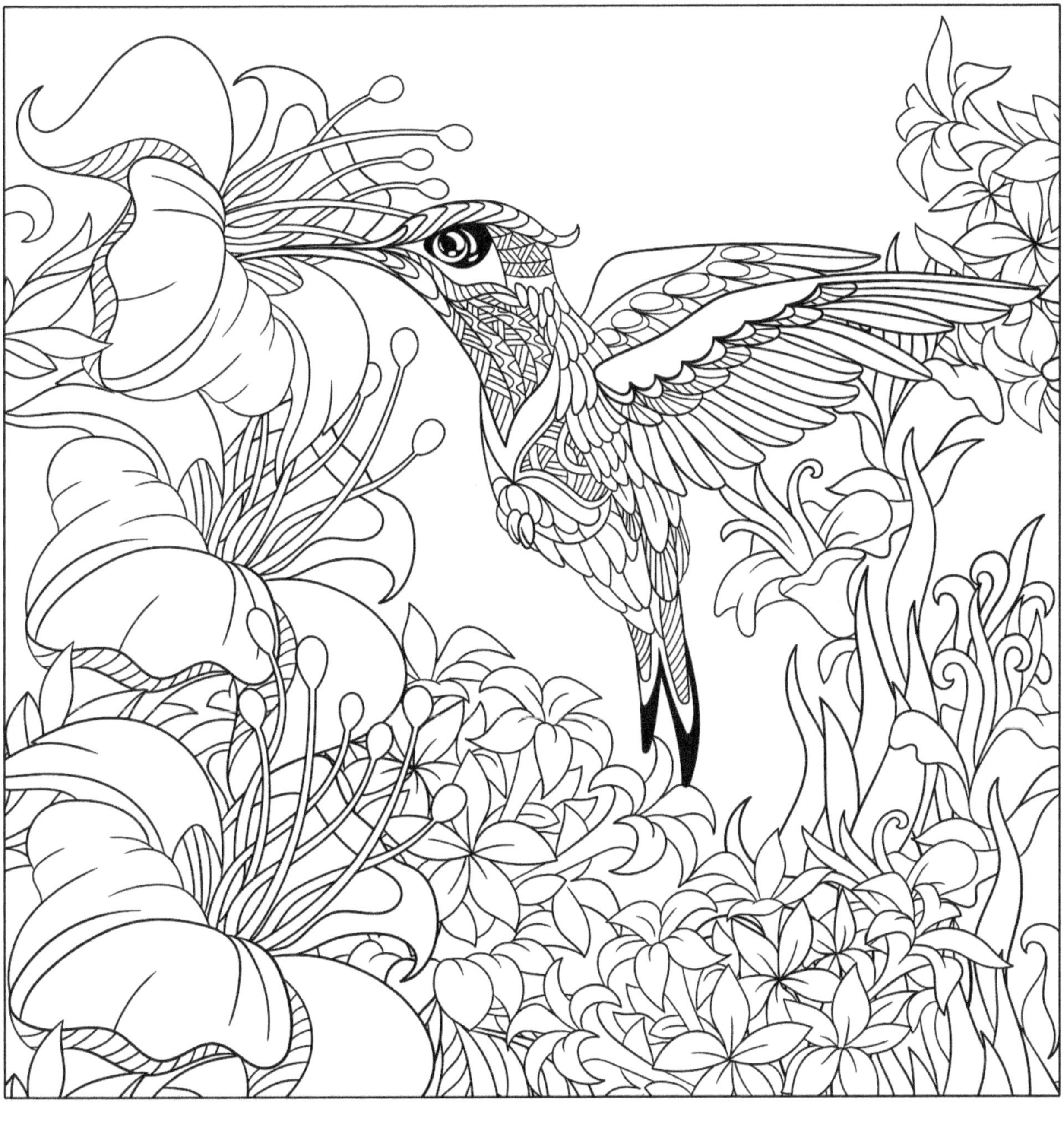

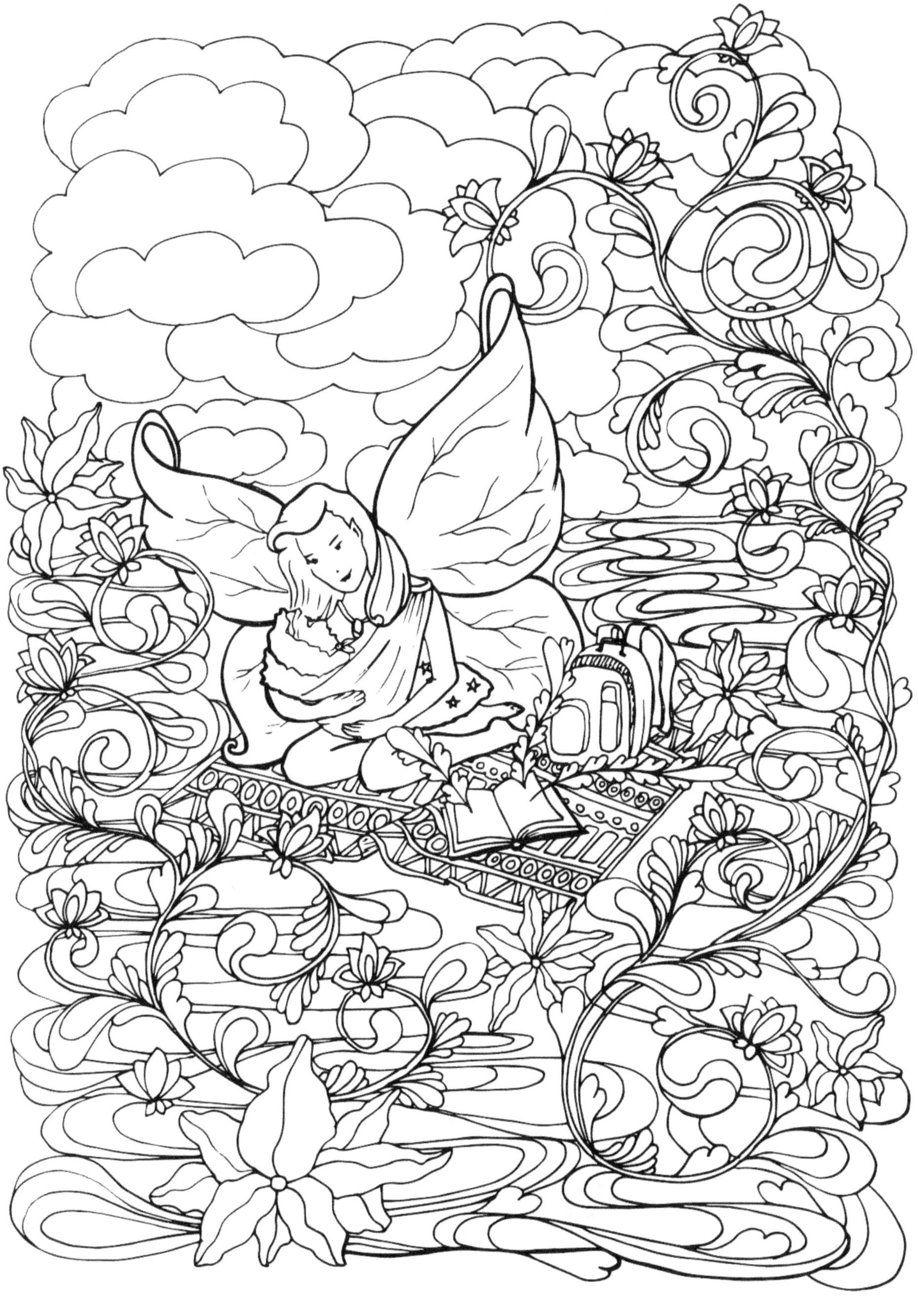

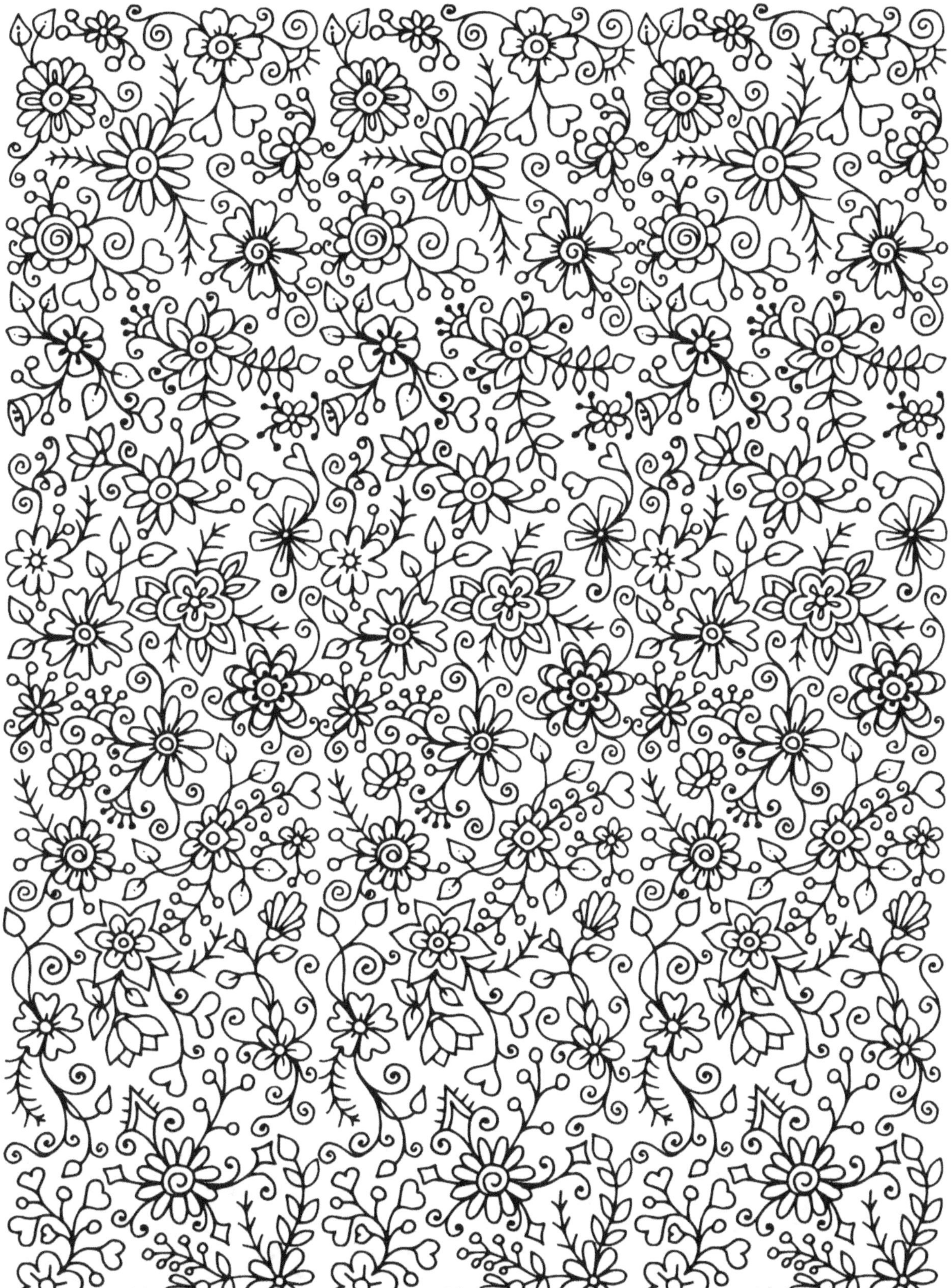

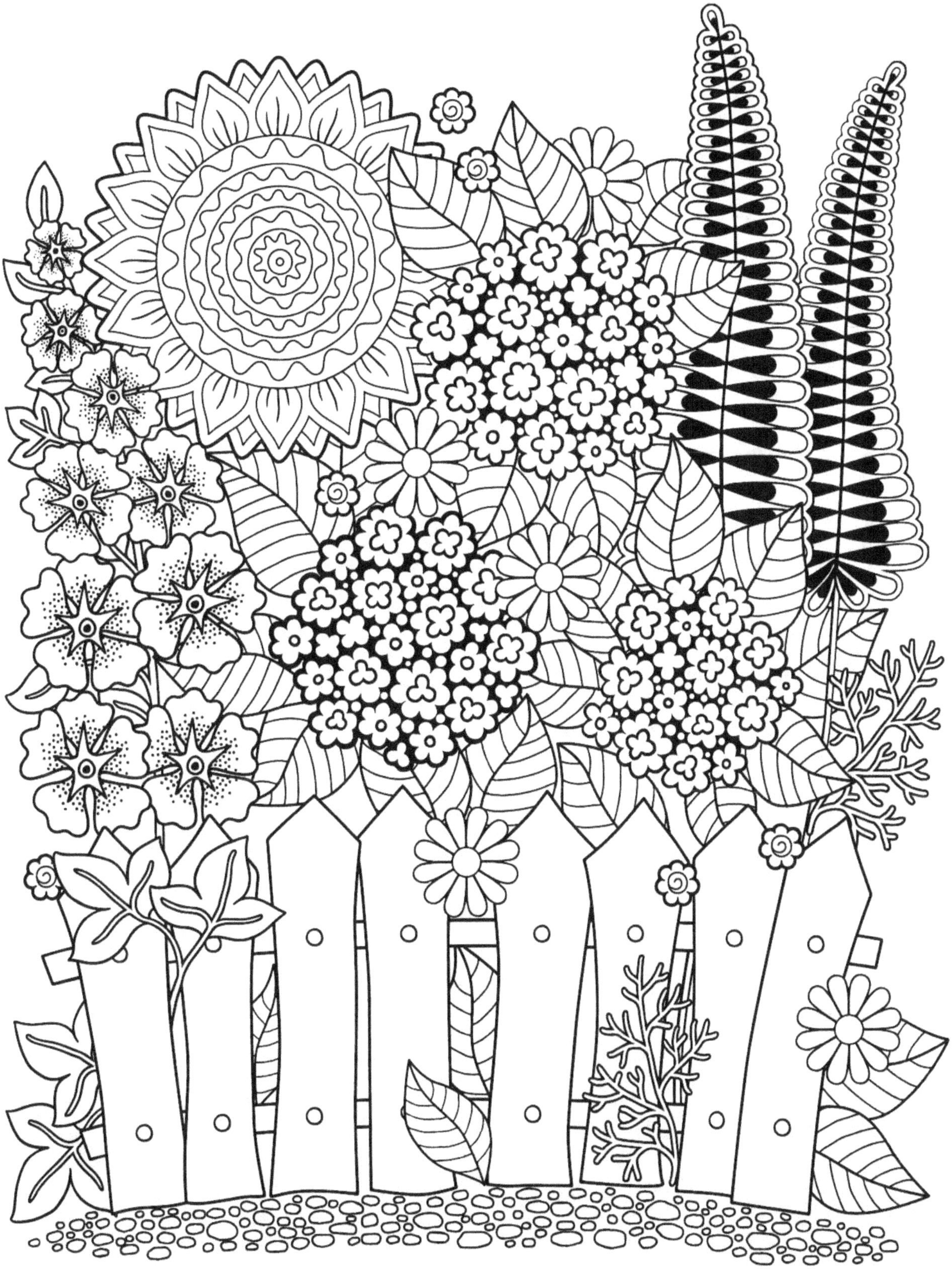

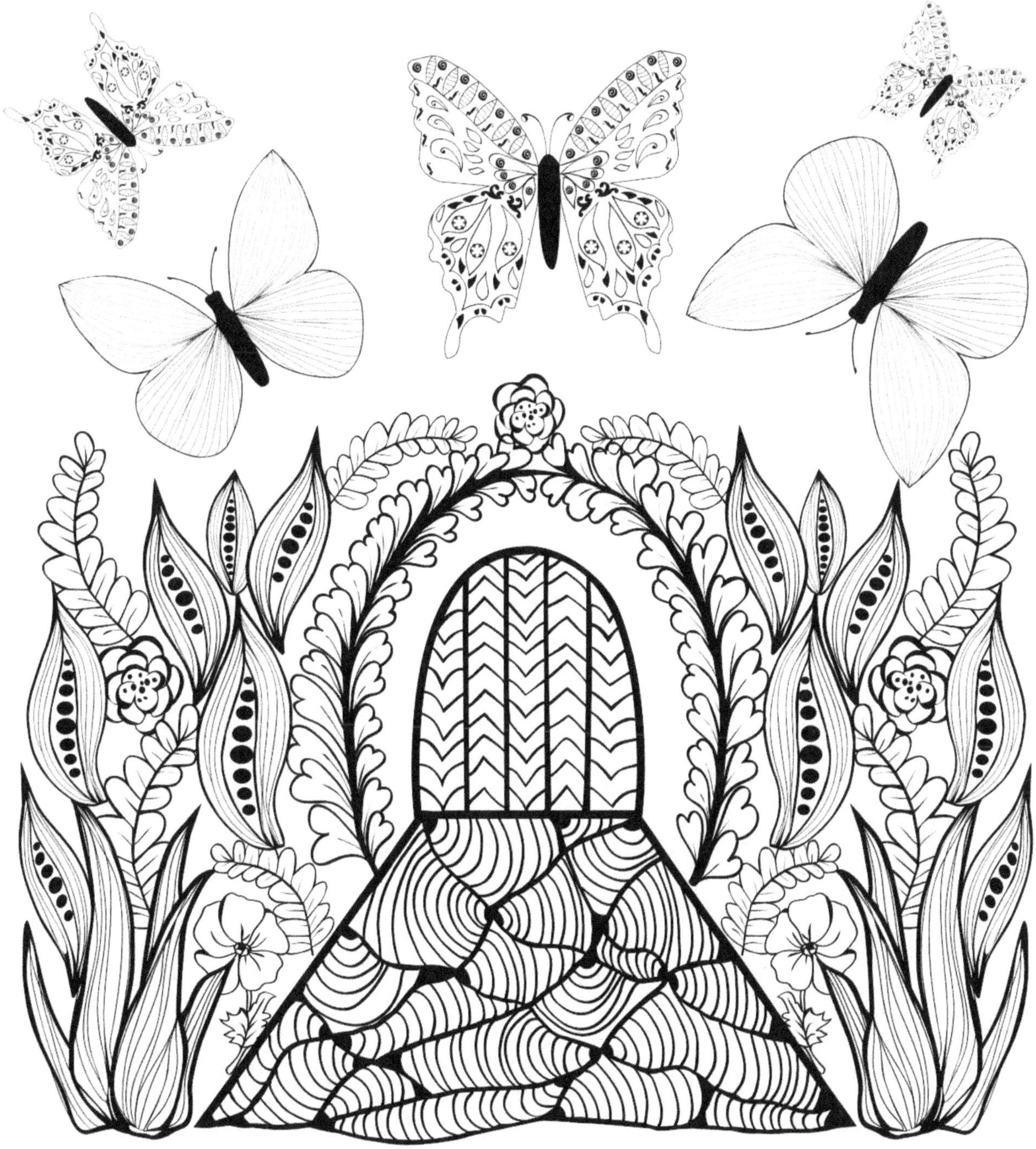

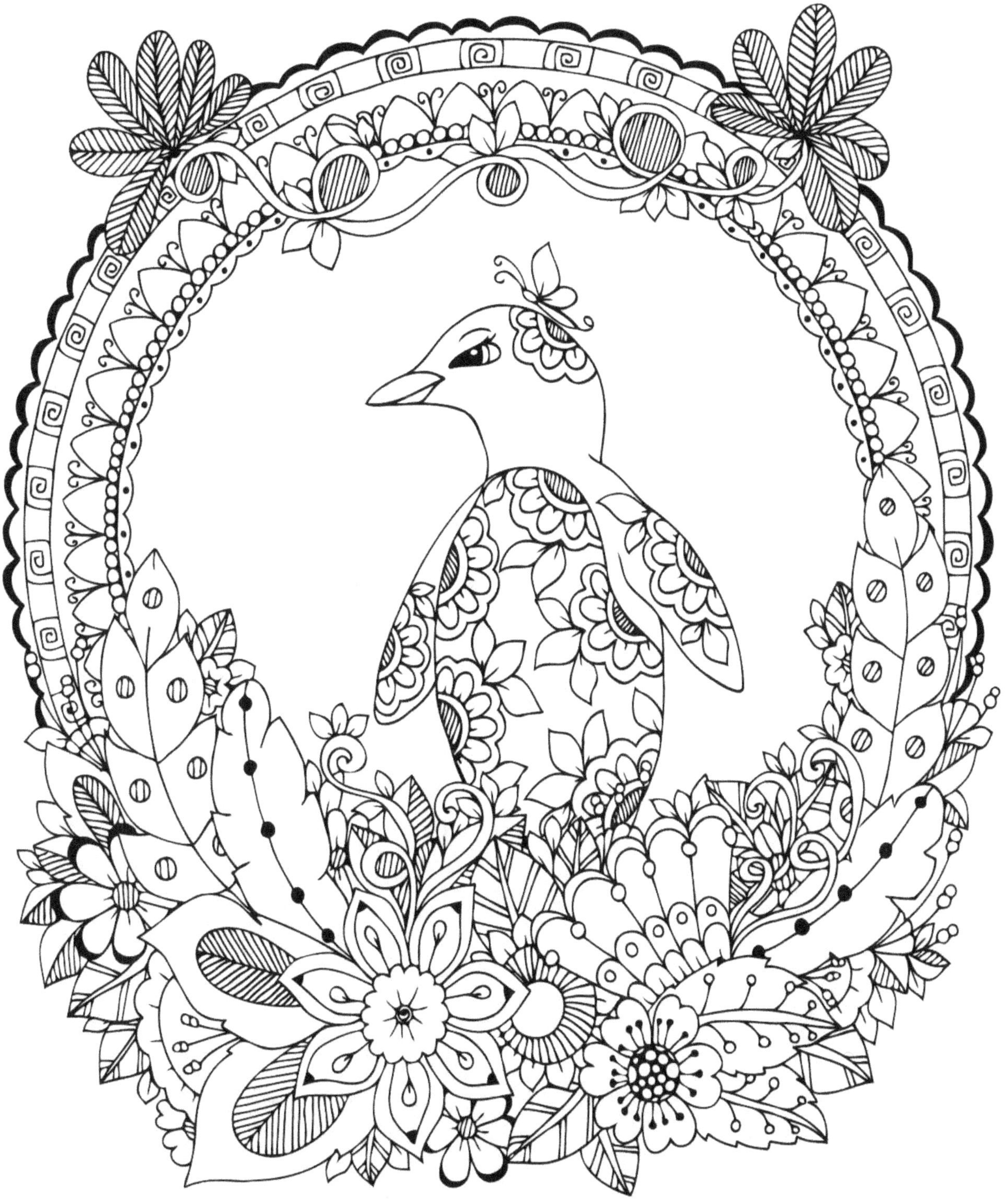

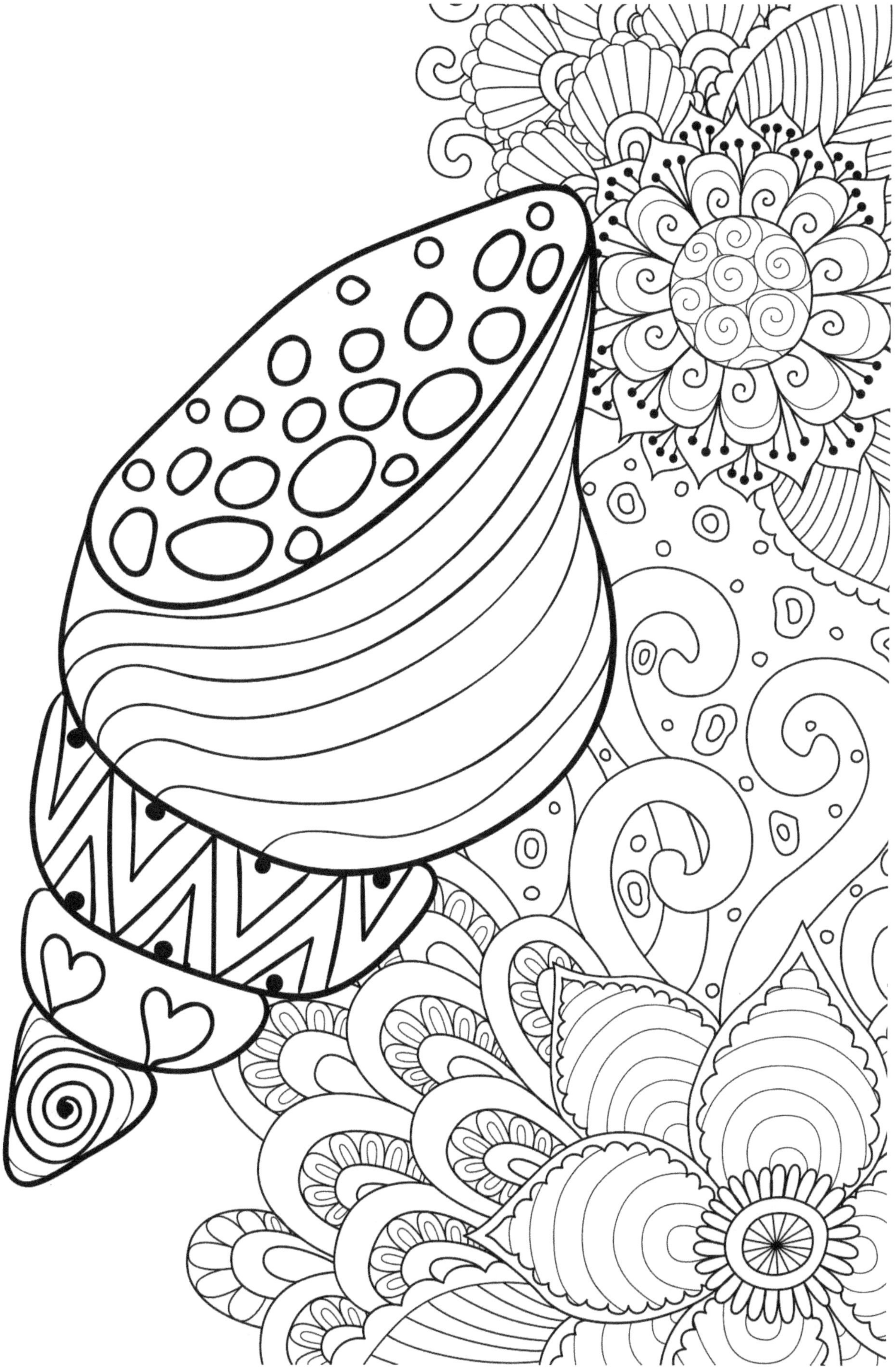

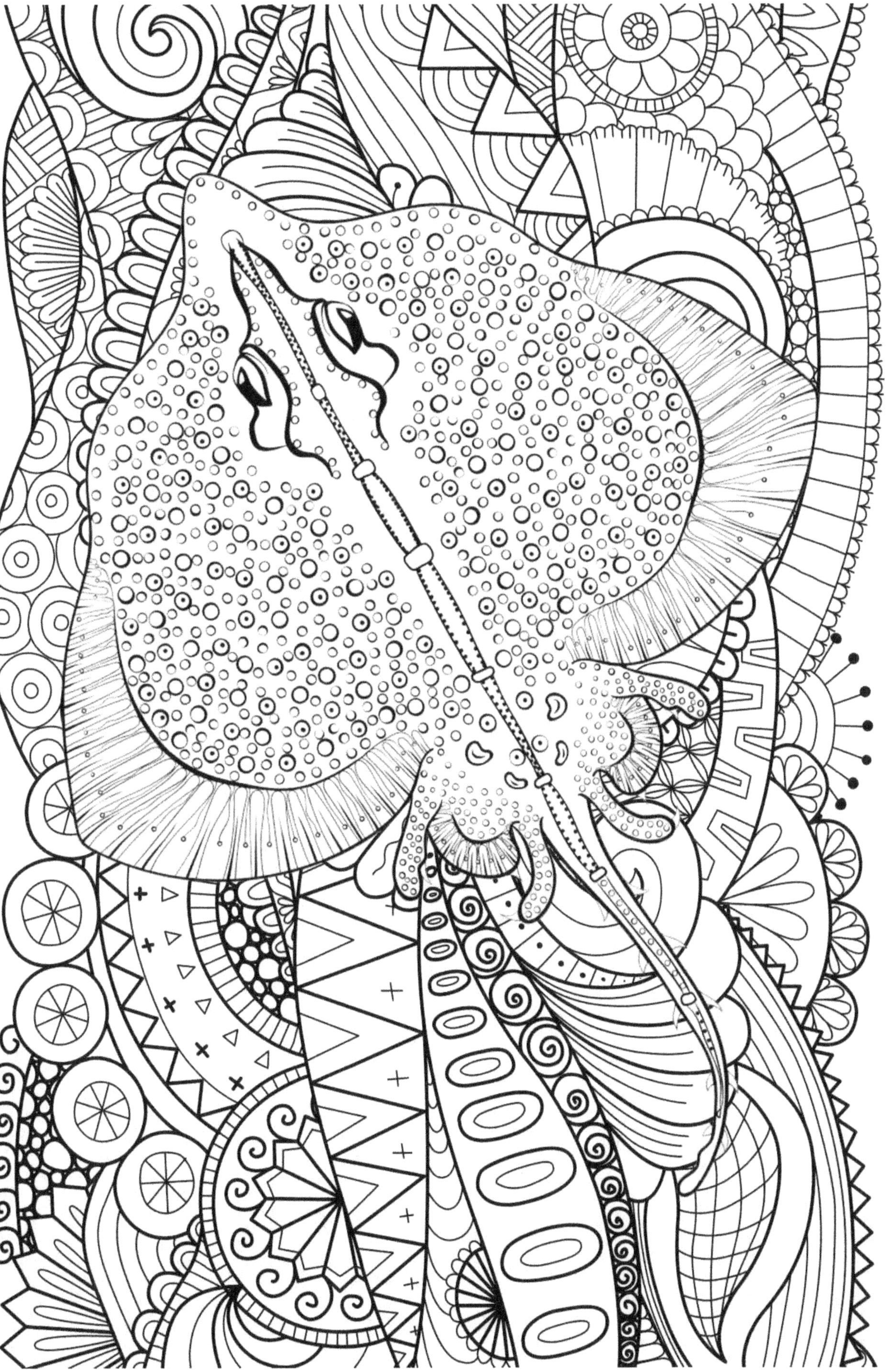

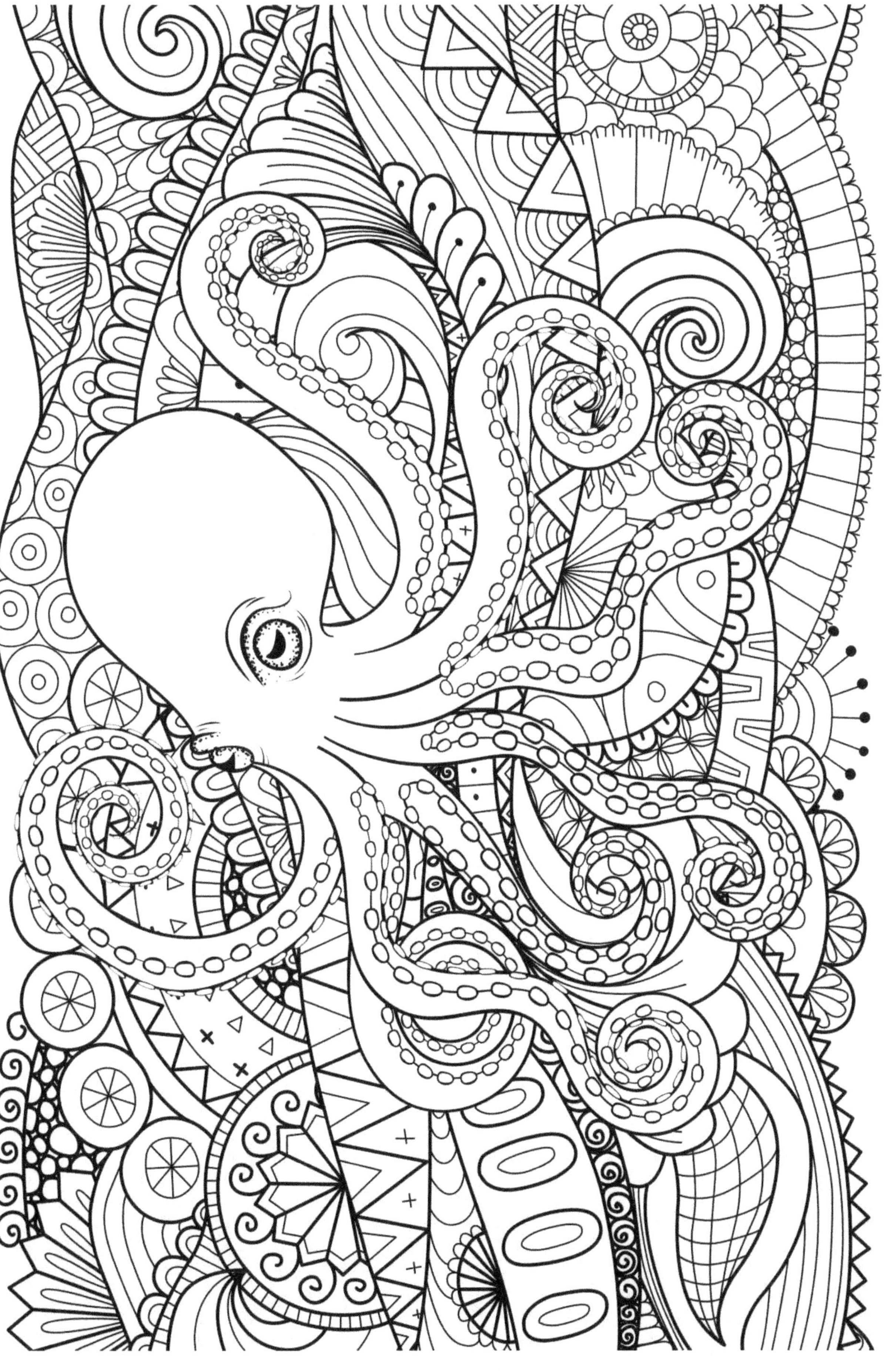

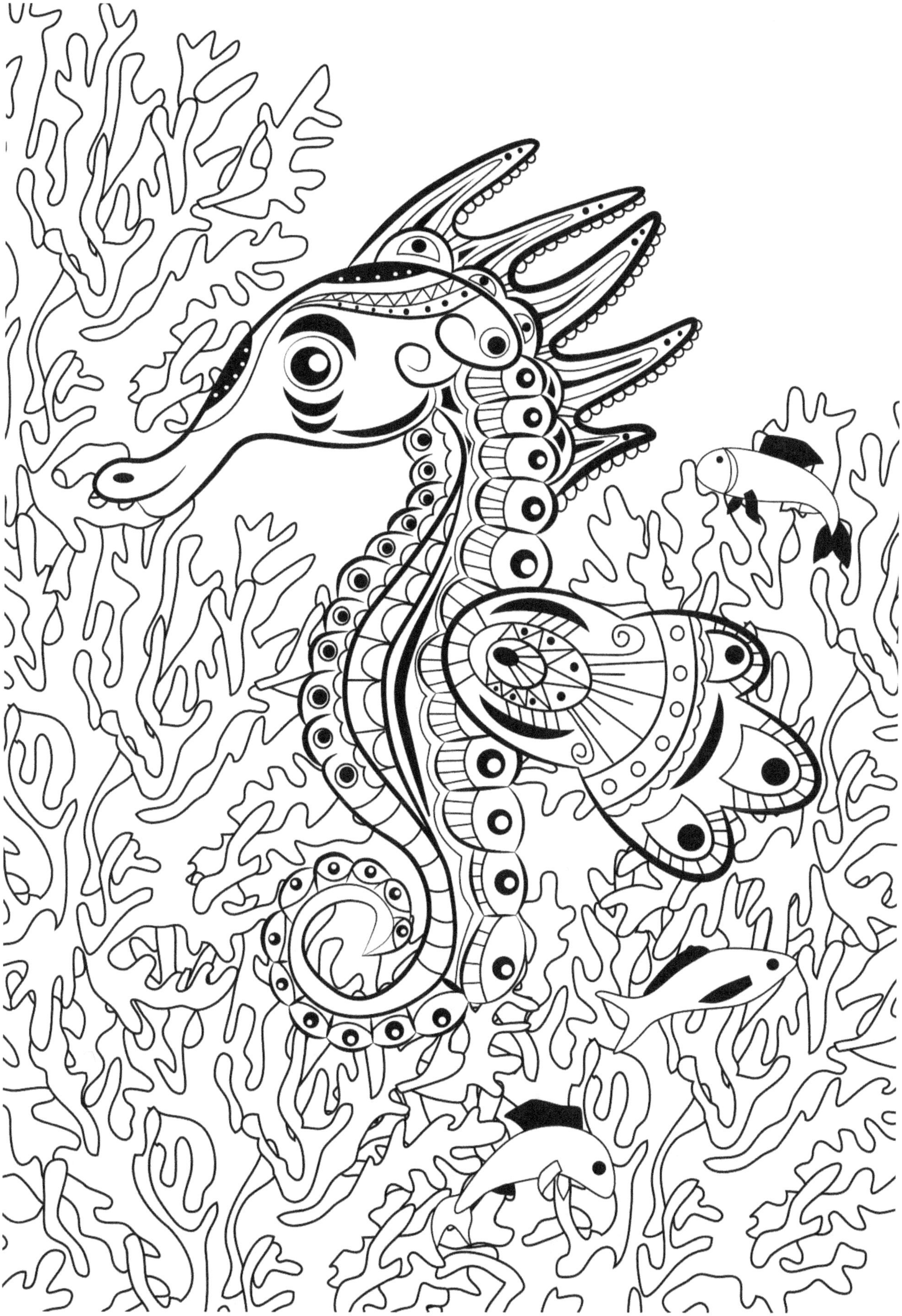

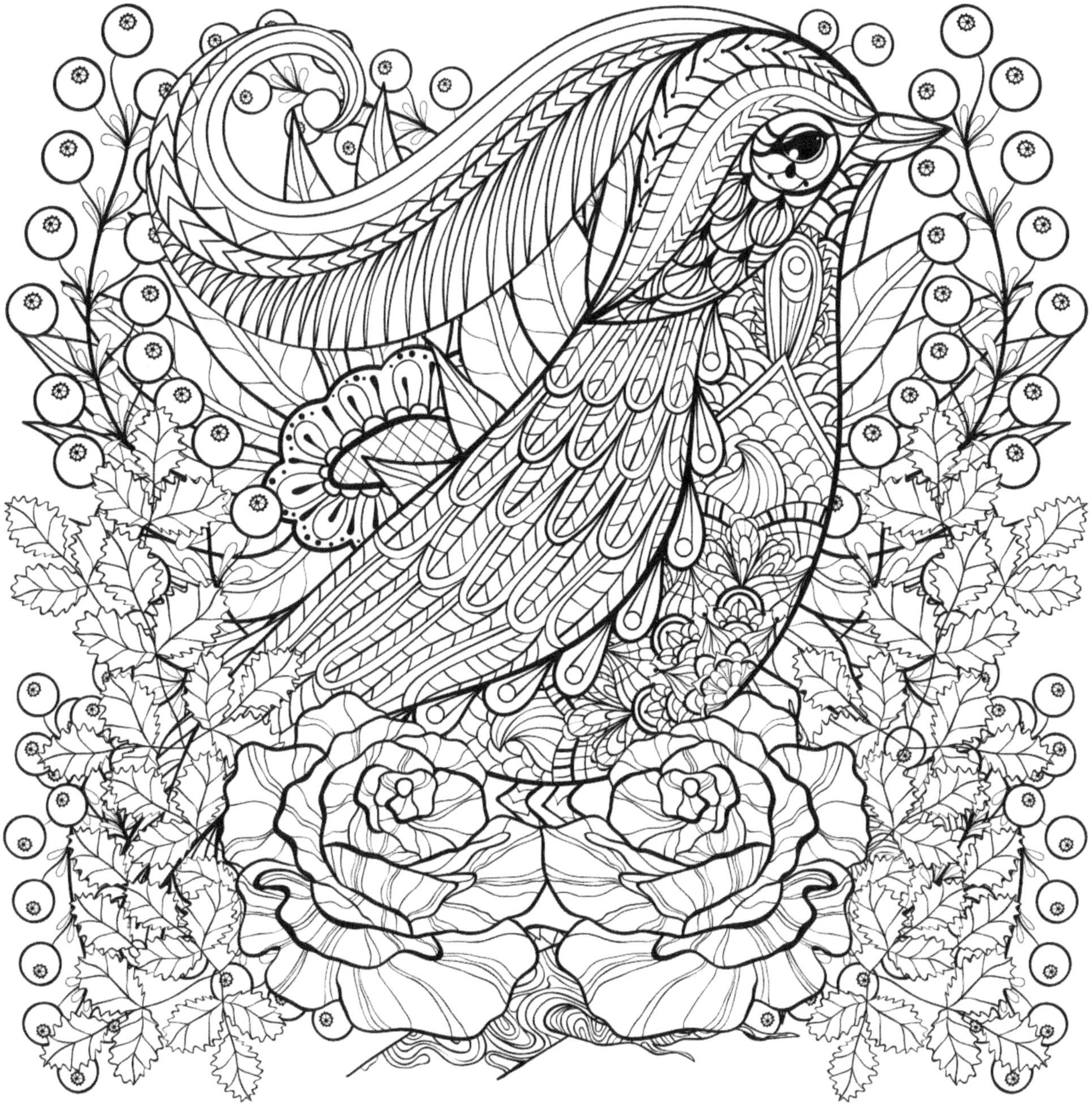

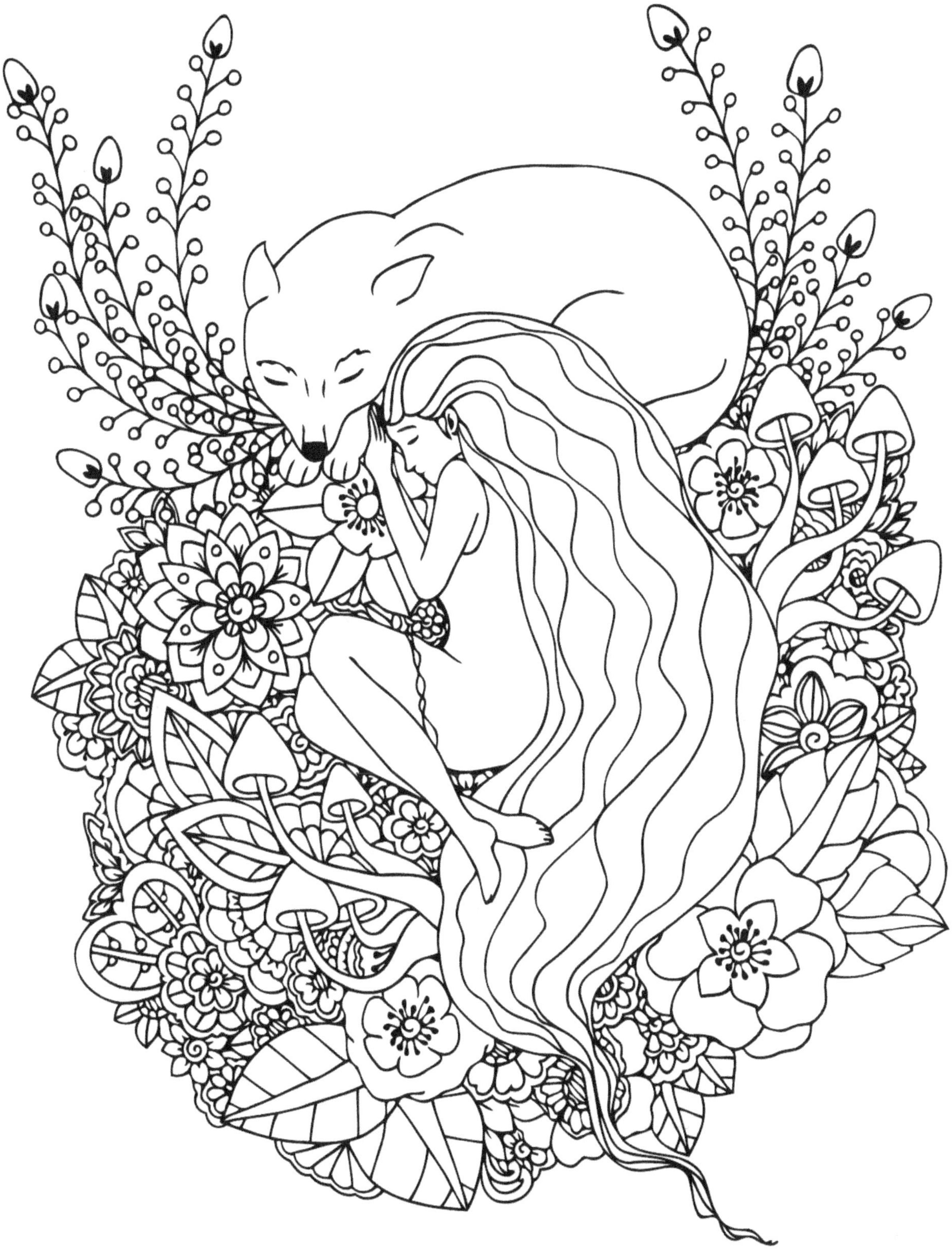

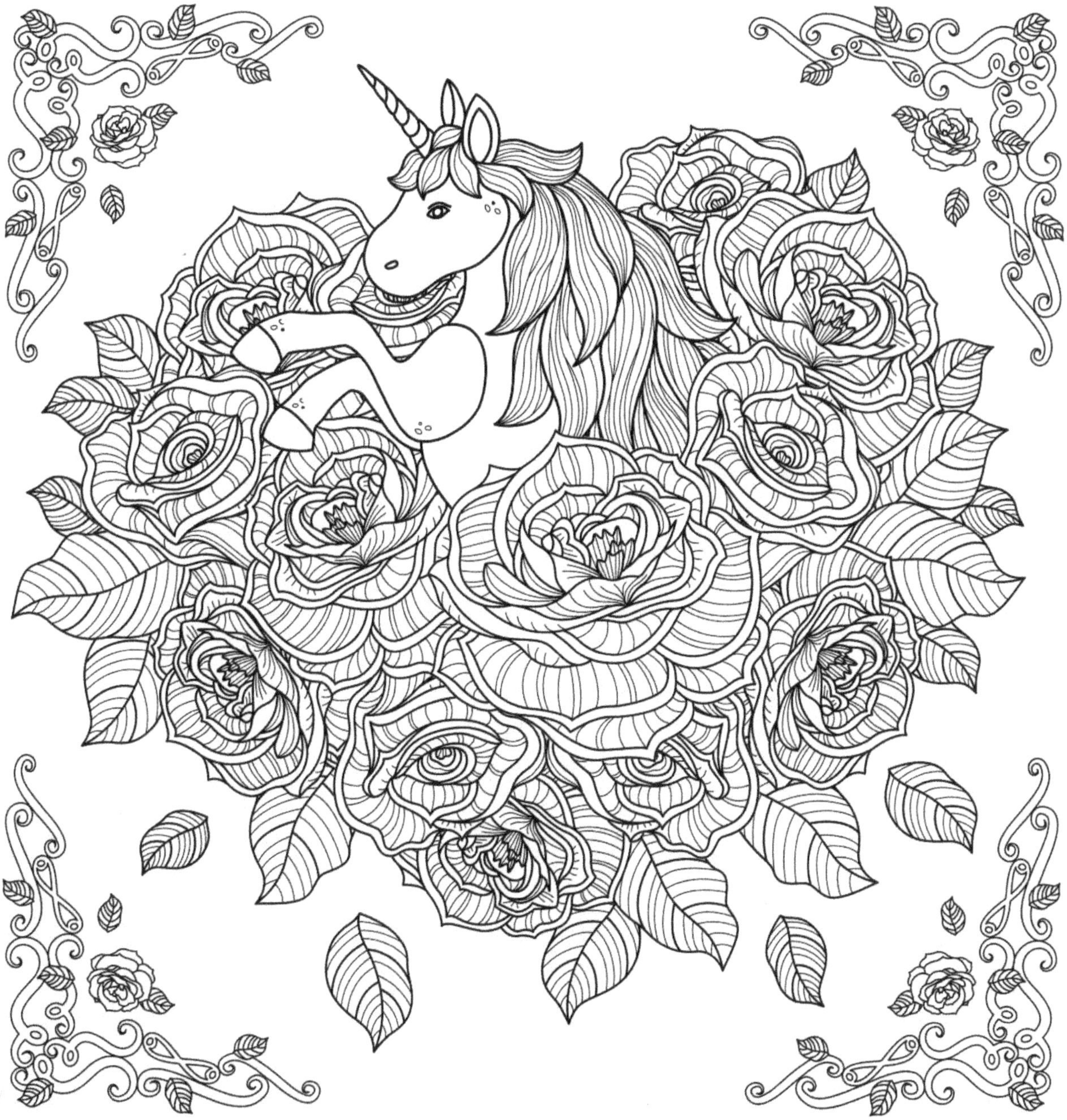

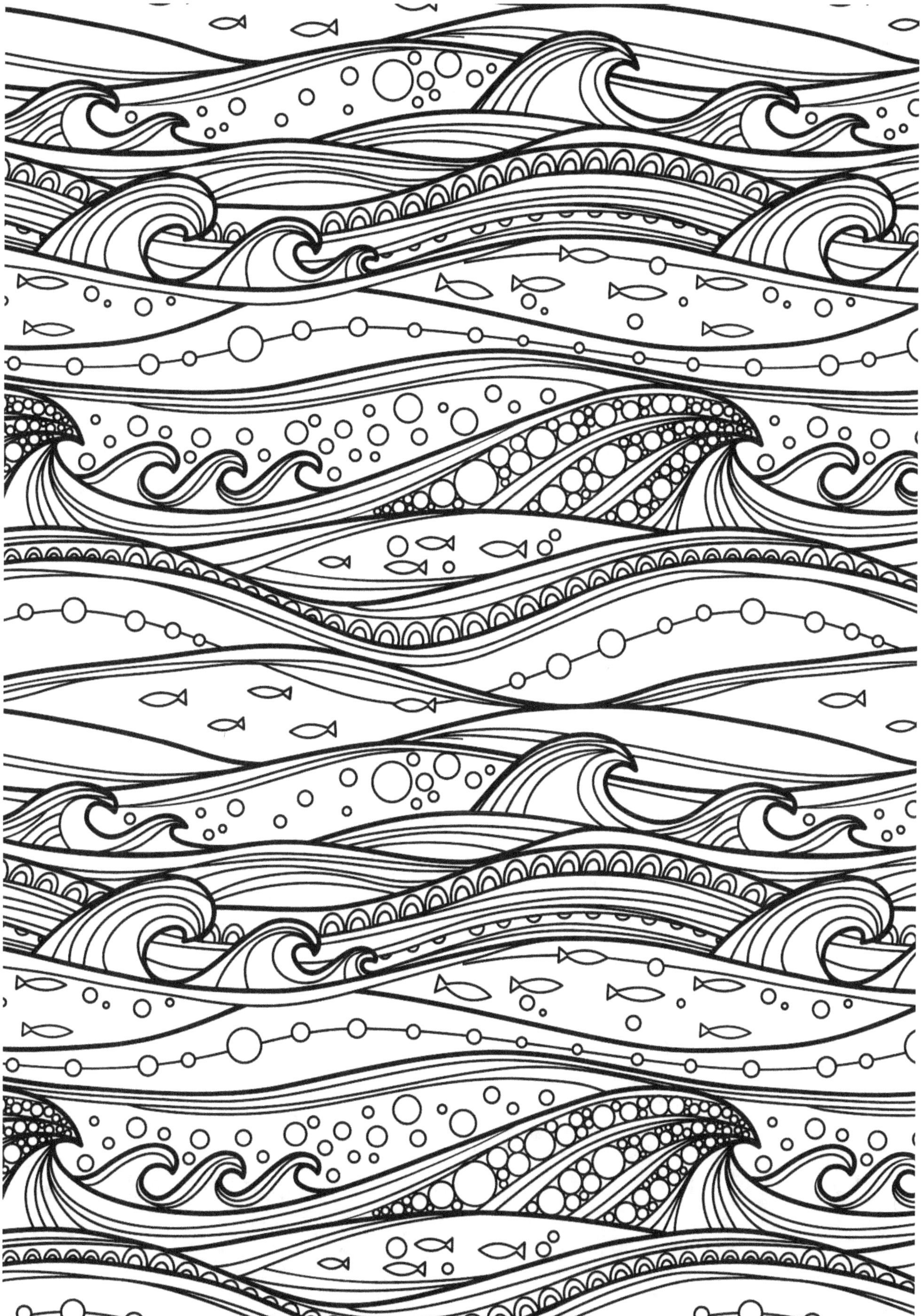

www.ingramcontent.com/pod-product-compliance
Lightning Source LLC
Chambersburg PA
CBHW081413280526
45788CB00009B/3087
* 9 7 8 1 5 4 2 8 2 9 9 7 7 *